THE SYMPHONIES
FOR ORGAN

RECENT RESEARCHES IN THE MUSIC OF THE NINETEENTH AND EARLY TWENTIETH CENTURIES

Rufus Hallmark, general editor

A-R Editions, Inc., publishes seven series of musicological editions
that present music brought to light in the course of current research:

Recent Researches in the Music of the Middle Ages and Early Renaissance
Charles Atkinson, general editor

Recent Researches in the Music of the Renaissance
James Haar, general editor

Recent Researches in the Music of the Baroque Era
Christoph Wolff, general editor

Recent Researches in the Music of the Classical Era
Eugene K. Wolf, general editor

Recent Researches in the Music of the Nineteenth and Early Twentieth Centuries
Rufus Hallmark, general editor

Recent Researches in American Music
H. Wiley Hitchcock, general editor

Recent Researches in the Oral Traditions of Music
Philip V. Bohlman, general editor

Each *Recent Researches* edition is devoted to works
by a single composer or to a single genre of composition.
The contents are chosen for their potential interest to scholars
and performers, then prepared for publication according to the
standards that govern the making of all reliable historical editions.

Subscribers to any of these series, as well as patrons of subscribing institutions,
are invited to apply for information about the "Copyright-Sharing Policy"
of A-R Editions, Inc., under which policy any part of an edition
may be reproduced free of charge for study or performance.

For information contact

A-R EDITIONS, INC.
801 Deming Way
Madison, Wisconsin 53717

(608) 836-9000

RECENT RESEARCHES IN THE MUSIC OF THE NINETEENTH
AND EARLY TWENTIETH CENTURIES • VOLUME 18

Charles-Marie Widor

THE SYMPHONIES FOR ORGAN

Symphonie VIII

Edited by John R. Near

A-R Editions, Inc.
Madison

Charles-Marie Widor
THE SYMPHONIES FOR ORGAN

Edited by John R. Near

*Recent Researches in the Music
of the Nineteenth and Early Twentieth Centuries*

Opus 13	Symphonie I	in C Minor	Volume 11
	Symphonie II	in D Major	Volume 12
	Symphonie III	in E Minor	Volume 13
	Symphonie IV	in F Minor	Volume 14
Opus 42	Symphonie V	in F Minor	Volume 15
	Symphonie VI	in G Minor	Volume 16
	Symphonie VII	in A Minor	Volume 17
	Symphonie VIII	in B Major	Volume 18
Opus 70	*Symphonie gothique*		Volume 19
Opus 73	*Symphonie romane*		Volume 20

© 1994 by A-R Editions, Inc.
All rights reserved
Printed in the United States of America

Library of Congress Cataloging-in-Publication Data

Widor, Charles Marie, 1844–1937.
 [Symphonies, organ, no. 8, op. 42, no. 4, B major]
 Symphonie VIII / edited by John R. Near.
 p. of music. — (The symphonies for organ / Charles-Marie Widor)
(Recent researches in the music of the nineteenth and early
twentieth centuries, ISSN 0193-5364 ; v. 18)
 "The original French editions and copies of these with corrections
and emendations in Widor's hand form the basis for this critical
edition"—P. vii.
 ISBN 0-89579-292-3
 1. Symphonies (Organ) I. Near, John Richard, 1947–.
II. Series. III. Series: Widor, Charles Marie, 1844–1937.
Symphonies, organ (A-R Editions)
M2.R23834 vol. 18
[M8]   93-49376
                                        CIP
                                         M

Contents

Introduction
   The Sources   vii
   Editorial Policies   viii
   Widor's Registrations   ix
   Critical Commentary   ix

Widor's *Avant-propos*   xvii

Symphonie VIII in B Major
   [I]   3
   II   18
   III   28
   IV. Variations   40
   V. Adagio   60
   VI. Finale   70

Appendix 1
   [I] Editions *B* and *B'*, Mm. 34–40, 52–56, 68–85, 135–38,
      146–52, 168–85, 215–20   84

Appendix 2
   III. Version *B/B'*, Mm. 229–49   90

Appendix 3
   IV. Prélude, Version *B/B'*   91

Appendix 4
   VII. Finale, Edition *B*, Mm. 261–69   94

Widor, 1901. Inscribed to Albert Riemenschneider and dated "Paris 1914," this photo of Widor at Saint-Sulpice is likely the one referred to by Madame Widor in a letter, 12 September 1928, to Albert Schweitzer: "I looked into the matter of photographs and am unable to succeed in obtaining a reproduction of the one taken in 1901 at the St. Sulpice organ. Granges [the photographer] is still in business, so one can't do anything aside from him" (Widor Correspondance, Maison Schweitzer, Gunsbach, France). This famous photo vividly evokes the description of Widor given by René Dumesnil (*Portraits de musiciens français,* p. 196): "Indeed, it was necessary to see Widor before the five manuals, pedal clavier, and stops—arranged in semicircles—of the great Saint-Sulpice organ. There, dominating some twenty meters above the nave that extended in front of the gigantic instrument, Widor was king. He reigned, and he had his court of musicians, the faithful, friends, and the inquisitive."

Courtesy The Riemenschneider Bach Institute
at Baldwin-Wallace College, Berea, Ohio

Introduction

From the time of their first publication, the organ symphonies of Charles-Marie Widor (1844–1937) have been recognized as masterpieces. Their influence on subsequent organ literature was once immense. As new generations of organ music became popular, however, there inevitably came a time when Widor's symphonies were neglected, often being judged outmoded. Even the French Romantic organ, perfected by Cavaillé-Coll and adored by musicians, was abused by later generations. Sufficient time was required to pass before Widor's art and instrument could be considered from a fresh and independent musical perspective. That perspective has evidently been achieved, for in recent years increasing numbers of musicians have begun evaluating the symphonies on their own terms, with the result that the works have enjoyed a notable resurgence of popularity. At the same time, the French Romantic organ has regained its former status.

Widor was perhaps his own most demanding critic. Following the first publication of each organ symphony, a continual transformation was effected by the composer through several revisions. In certain cases nearly six decades intervened between first and last versions of a work. Even after the final published edition, Widor continued to scrutinize his organ works, applying finishing touches to the pieces that have constituted his most enduring legacy.

This comprehensive edition of Widor's ten organ symphonies is the first to incorporate the many final emendations made by the composer in his own copies. Here also are presented for the first time together substantially or completely different earlier versions of passages, sections, and complete movements as they were conceived by Widor in the course of his long career. Using information in the Critical Commentary and the music of the Appendixes, musicians can perform or study these several earlier versions of each work.

The Preface to this edition (vol. 1, Symphonie I) provides a full discussion of the symphonies' genesis and historical environment as well as an extended discussion of editorial policy, sources, and performance. In this Introduction are provided information on performance sufficient to give the reader a sense of Widor's own preferences in registration and expression (including a translation of his foreword, or *avant-propos*), a conspectus of the sources, a summary of editorial policy, and a Critical Commentary.

The Sources

The original French editions and copies of these with corrections and emendations in Widor's hand form the basis for this critical edition. The locations of Widor's original holographs, if extant, are unknown. After extensively researching these works, the editor believes that all editions have surfaced, with one possible exception, noted in the Preface. These are listed here together with the identifying abbreviations used in the Critical Commentary and Appendixes. (More complete information on the sources appears in the Preface to the present edition.)

A   The first edition of opus 13, Symphonies I–IV, published in Paris in 1872 by the firm of J. Maho.

A'   A subsequent issue of *A* with minuscule alterations, published in 1879 by the firm of J. Hamelle together with the first editions of Symphonies V and VI.

B   The first complete issue of opus 42, comprising Symphonies V–VIII, together with the first major revision of opus 13, published in Paris in 1887 by Hamelle.

B'   A subsequent issue of *B* with small revisions to Symphonies I, VI, VII, and VIII, released between 1888 and 1892.

C   A new edition of opuses 13 and 42 (excepting Symphonie VI), published in 1901 and bearing the heading "New edition, revised, and entirely modified by the composer (1900–1901)."

C'   A subsequent issue of *C* that includes a new version of Symphonie VI and revisions to Symphonies I–V and VII–VIII, released by 1911.

D   A new edition of opuses 13 and 42, published in 1920, bearing the heading "New edition, revised, and entirely modified by the composer (1914–1918), (1920)."

E   The final published edition, again with revisions, issued 1928–29.

Emend 1   A copy of *B'* apparently used by Widor while preparing the revisions of edition *C* but also containing other emendations.

Emend 2   A bound and complete collection of single symphonies (representing variously the versions of editions *D* or *E*) with emendations made by Widor mostly after 1929, the year of edition *E*.

Emend 3   A copy of Symphonie V in the version of edition *D*, with numerous emendations by the composer, dated October 1927 in Widor's hand. This copy includes the revisions present in the 1929 edition, but it also contains further emendations, including some duplicated in *Emend* 2 and arguably entered after 1929.

Riem 8   Berea, Ohio, The Riemenschneider Bach Institute at Baldwin-Wallace College, R 4008, includes a single copy of Symphonie VIII in edition C.

Schw 7–8 Gunsbach, France, Maison Schweitzer, MO 158, a bound volume of Symphonies VII (movements V–VI) and VIII. This copy, which represents edition C, has no markings for Symphonie VIII except a marginal note on the first page of the last movement; this is discussed in the critical commentary.

Identical versions of movements in different editions are denoted in the Critical Commentary and the Appendixes by a slash between the identifying letters; for example, *A/A'/B/B'* means that a movement so identified remains the same through editions *A, A', B,* and *B'*.

Editorial Policies

Edition *E* (or, what amounts to the same thing, a version remaining constant through edition *E*) is generally taken as the principal source for the main body of this edition. Sources for Appendix variants are identified individually in the Critical Commentary. All departures from the source either are distinguished typographically (when they are editorial and straightforward) or are identified in the Critical Commentary (when they derive from other sources or are not explained by policies described here). There are two exceptions to the policy of bracketing: editorial ties, slurs, hairpins, and directs are dashed; editorial cautionary accidentals appear in reduced size; all other editorial additions are enclosed in brackets.

The original French prints are themselves replete with cautionary accidentals, usually provided to cancel flats and sharps in previous measures. All except repetitious cautionary accidentals within a measure are preserved in this edition.

In the Critical Commentary the three staves of a system are indexed 1, 2, and 3, in order from top to bottom. Occasionally staff 1 in the source editions is congested, while an empty or nearly empty staff lies directly below. In such contexts this edition sometimes tacitly transfers left-hand voices to the open staff 2.

In the sources, indications of dynamics under staff 1 are sometimes duplicated under staves 2 or 3 or both in contexts where the Pédale and other manuals would have to share those dynamics in any event. The editor has suppressed most of these redundant dynamic indications. In addition, the old engravings frequently place dynamic indications over staff 1 because of space limitations on the page; conversely, they sometimes place tempo indications between staves 1 and 2 for the same reason. This edition tacitly regularizes the position of all such marks, putting dynamic indications within the system and tempo indications above it. There is an obvious exception to this rule: namely, when a dynamic is meant to apply to one staff alone, it appears closest to the affected voice(s)—therefore, sometimes above staff 1. Because Widor indicated registration and dynamics somewhat differently in editions *A* and *A'*, the source placement of the relevant signs is preserved in appendix extracts from them.

Widor indicated staccato with the dot up to the late 1890s, but he favored the wedge thereafter. The two signs become mixed in passages partially revised by the composer after about 1900 (the period of edition *C*). Widor's pedagogical works on organ music reveal that both signs had the same significance for him. In the present edition all wedges are tacitly changed to dots in pieces conceived before Widor's change of orthography; wedges are retained in movements composed after the change.

Beaming in the original French editions is sometimes used to clarify phrasing. Beaming in the new edition follows that of the sources except when, under certain stringent conditions spelled out in detail in the Preface to this edition (see vol. 11, Symphonie I), it can be shown with great probability that inconsistencies arise through oversight or through adherence to an outmoded convention for beaming.

Characteristic of Widor's musical orthography is its attention to inner contrapuntal voices in every musical texture. At times this leads to a phalanx of stems all aiming for the same metrical position. Stemming in the new edition generally follows that of the sources, since the appearance of counterpoint, even in predominantly homophonic textures, conveys much of the "feel" and attitude proper to Widor's symphonies. Departures from the source are made only in clearly defined circumstances spelled out in detail in the Preface to this edition. In general, the number of voices in a measure is kept constant. In clearly homophonic contexts, where Widor himself is less strict, inconsistencies in the number of voices in a measure are usually allowed to stand. All editorial rests are bracketed. Stems added by analogy with parallel or closely similar passages are not bracketed, but the source reading is reported in a critical note. All other stems added to clarify inconsistent voicing are bracketed. Infrequently, superfluous rests or stems in the sources are tacitly removed to keep part writing consistent in a measure.

In conformity with accepted practice of that era, the original French editions of Widor's organ symphonies provide double barlines for all changes of key and for some changes of meter. In this edition these are converted to single barlines unless there is also a new tempo, a new texture, or some other sign of a structural subdivision.

Reference to pitch in the Critical Commentary is made as follows: middle C = c'; C above middle C = c''; C below middle C = c; two octaves below middle

C = C. Successive pitches are separated by commas, simultaneous pitches by virgules.

Widor's Registrations

Widor generally indicated registrations by family of tone-color instead of exact stop nomenclature. In so doing he never intended to condone willful or indiscriminate interpretations of his registrational plans. He had a particular horror of kaleidoscopic stop changes and artlessly haphazard use of the Expression pedal. To those who indulged in a continual manipulation of the stops or Expression pedal, he habitually advised, "I beg you, no magic lantern effects." Barring the unfortunate necessity of making certain adaptations to varying organs, one should no more alter the "orchestration" of a Widor organ symphony than change or dress up the instrumentation of a Beethoven symphony. Clearly, the faithful realization of Widor's registrational plan is essential to the presentation of these works as the composer heard them. Beyond this, knowledge of the Cavaillé-Coll organ, the instrument preferred by Widor, will also prove useful to the performer intent on maximum fidelity to the composer's intention. A discussion of this organ and its constraints on performance can be found in the Preface to this edition (see vol. 11, Symphonie I).

To indicate the registration he wanted, Widor adopted a relatively simple shorthand system: **G** represents Grand-orgue (Great); **P** Positif (Positive); **R** Récit (Swell); **Péd.** Pédale (Pedal). Fonds are the foundation stops; Anches the chorus reed stops as well as all correlative stops included in the Jeux de combinaison. Pitch designations are self-evident.

When found above, within, or directly below the keyboard staves, a single letter instructs the organist to play on that particular uncoupled manual. When two or three letters are combined in these locations, the first designates the manual to play on, the second and subsequent letters what is to be coupled to it. For example, **GPR** instructs the organist to play on the Grand-orgue with the Positif and Récit coupled to it; **PR** tells one to play on the Positif with the Récit coupled to it; and so on.

When found under the lowest staff, one or more letters designate which manuals are to be coupled to the Pédale. When Widor employs only a dynamic marking in the course of the Pédale line, the performer should determine at his own discretion which Pédale coupler needs to be retired or reintroduced.

All crescendo and decrescendo indications, no matter how lengthy, are to be effected only by manipulation of the Expression pedal, unless the crescendo leads to a *fff*. In that case the Jeux de combinaison of each division are to be brought into play successively on strong beats: first those of the Récit (perhaps already on), then those of the Positif (sometimes indicated with a *ff*), and finally those of the Grand-orgue and Pédale on the *fff*. For the decrescendo they are to be retired in reverse order on weak beats.

Critical Commentary

In scale and design this big, expansive work is fully on a par with many of the late-Romantic orchestral symphonies. Certainly, no more monumental organ composition had previously been conceived: the seven movements of the original edition fill sixty-seven pages of score and require about one hour to perform. As Camille Saint-Saëns once wrote to Widor, "the great majority of organists . . . are not of your powers and . . . recoil, terrified, before your works."[*] Concentrating his highest conceptual capacities on this symphony, which he himself described as having "severity at first sight,"[†] Widor must have felt that he had pushed organ technique to the limit and exhausted the tonal possibilities of the instrument. More than a fitting climax to opus 42, this was to be the capstone to his organ works. The great master of the organ symphony fully intended to write no more organ music.[‡] Symphonie VIII exists in four versions: *B, B', C,* and *C'/D/E*.

[I]

Widor's approach to the musical organization of his first movements is nontraditional throughout the organ symphonies. In these works, at least, he eschewed the familiar sonata principle that generations of composers had led listeners to anticipate. This spacious movement begins in the most compact manner: a two-measure introduction presents a motive which springs up a tenth and then falls back an octave. The composer seems to be alerting us to the movement's three impending upward-pointing main themes (mm. 3, 56, and 71). In the first theme group, the principal idea traces an angular outline ending with the upward leap of a tenth; in the second theme group, an upward scalar motive spans an eleventh; and in the third theme group, the melody climbs haltingly through an octave. The originality of the movement's design is noteworthy. After the thematic exposition, musical materials from each theme group are freely developed in rondolike succession: A group, m. 84; B group, m. 117; A group, m. 149; C group, m. 168; A group, m. 182; Coda (A), m. 218. Along the way developmental techniques such as inversion, augmentation, fragmentation, and intermingling of melodic and motivic elements help build a strong, coherent musical entity.

This movement, in a symphony where relatively few revisions were effected, received a number of important modifications. There are four versions: *B, B', C,* and

---

[*]Paris, Institut de France, "Lettres adressées à Widor de Saint-Saëns," number 54, dated 29 September 1919.

[†]Letter dated 10 April 1887, editor's collection. For a more complete text of this letter, see the Critical Commentary to Symphonie VII.

[‡]Henry Eymieu, *Études et biographies musicales* (Paris: Fischerbacher, 1892), 15.

C'/D/E. The readings of the variant measures in editions B and B' are given as Appendix 1; the minor variants between versions C and C'/D/E are reported below. Widor made no marks on this symphony in *Emend* 2 (version C'/D/E). For the final version, edition E is the principal source.

Edition C differs from version C'/D/E as follows. Mm. 78–79 have no *meno vivo* directive. Mm. 81–83 are compressed into two measures with differing tempo directives, shown in example 1. M. 147 (m. 146 in C), staff 1, beat 1, chord is d"-sharp/f"[-sharp]/d'''-sharp.

Example 1. I, mm. 81–83, as they appear in edition C (m. 83 = m. 84 in C'/D/E).

In *Emend* 1 (edition B') of this movement, numerous revisions, sketches, and some indecipherable scribblings appear variously in orange, blue, and black pencil, and in black ink. A few revisions shown in *Emend* 1 were made without modification in C; some seem to be intermediary sketches, which appear with further changes in C; still others were not used at all. Widor evidently changed his mind about the latter.

In the interest of comparison with the final version, unequivocal emendations in *Emend* 1 that were not used in C are given here. (Because of deleted measures, measure numbers between versions differ; those given refer to the analogous measures in the present edition.) M. 37, staff 2, upper voice, notes 3 and 4 are a'[-sharp]. Mm. 38 and 39, staff 2, the second dyad—and consequently the fourth—is g'-double sharp/b'-sharp. M. 54, staff 2, lower voice is d-sharp dotted quarter note tied to d[-sharp] eighth note—two eighth rests would also be needed. M. 68, staff 2, note 1 has **PR** directive. M. 200, staff 2, note 2 is f'[-sharp] eighth note, note 3 is c"[-sharp] eighth note—possibly this is intended to be quarter note since there is an eighth rest over staff 3, note 1. M. 216, staff 2, beat 1 is a-natural slurred with f[-sharp], e-sharp, f[-sharp], a[-natural], d'-natural (with trill) sixteenth notes; beat 2 is f'[-sharp] slurred with e'-sharp, f'[-sharp], a'[-natural], d"-natural (with trill), e"-natural (with trill) sixteenth notes. M. 217, staff 2, beat 1 is f"[-sharp] eighth note, two eighth rests; nothing is shown for beat 2.

CRITICAL NOTES

M. 37, staff 2, upper voice, note 4 has no eighth flag in C and C'/D/E—an error. M. 43, staff 2 has no tie in C and C'/D/E—m. 44, which begins another system and page, has an incoming tie from m. 43, and the tie conforms to analogous m. 202.

M. 50, staff 1, the caesura appears in editions C, C', and D—it likely faded from the available pressings of edition E. M. 54, beat 1 has *a tempo* in all editions; this directive should have been deleted when *poco allargando* was deleted from m. 52 in edition C. M. 56, Widor often provides double barlines as a sign of structural subdivision (cf. mm. 3 and 218); one seems especially appropriate here with the commencement of the second theme group (for further information, see Editorial Procedures, "Barlines" in vol. 1 of this series). Mm. 56–57 and 60–61, staff 2, slurs follow analogous mm. 117–18 and 121–22. Mm. 77–78, staff 1, editorial extension of slur follows analogous mm. 174–75. M. 81, staff 1, beat 1, chord 2, f[-sharp] has natural in *Riem* 8—the editor questions the early arrival of f-natural because it results in an exact repetition in beat 2. M. 86, staff 1, editorial tie conforms to B and B' and to incoming tie in m. 87, which begins another system—the tie was inadvertently omitted when the system was reengraved for C. M. 95, staff 3 has superfluous eighth rest aligned under staff 2, note 3, in all editions—an error.

M. 115, staff 2, beat 1, chord has superfluous tie on top note in C and C'/D/E—this should have been deleted when m. 114 was revised for C; *a tempo* follows B/B' reading of analogous m. 54 (see report there)—the lack of the directive here is undoubtedly due to an oversight that occurred when *allargando* was added to m. 114 in C. M. 133, hairpin follows placement in analogous m. 145. M. 134, staff 3, beat 2, note 3, upper voice is quarter note—eighth flag follows analogous m. 146, which was revised from upstemmed quarter note in C. M. 135, staff 3, upper voice, note 6 is g'-natural in B'—a correction from g'[-sharp] in B—the rising chromatic line and harmonic implication seem to indicate that the accidental was deleted in error when the system was reengraved with revisions for C. M. 137, beat 1 has *a tempo* in all editions—m. 136, staff 3, beat 2 has *poco ritard.* in B and B', conforming to the analogous *rit.* in m. 148; assuming the directive was correctly deleted from m. 136 in C, the retention of *a tempo* in m. 137 was an oversight; this appears to be one of several instances where Widor deleted a tempo directive, fearing that too many could cause undue exaggeration on the performer's part (see Widor's *Avant-propos*, par. 8).

M. 182, staff 3, beat 2, slur follows editions B and B' and similar m. 184—when staff 3 was revised for C, no articulation was given here, though m. 183 (on the next system) continued to show an incoming slur; also note the articulation of m. 184, staff 3, beat 1, which may be appropriate to m. 182 as well. M. 183, staff 2, editorial slur continues outgoing slur of m. 182. M. 185, staff 3, note 6, sharp follows *Riem* 8 and seems correct in the ascending pattern. M. 199, staff 1, upper note has superfluous tie in addition to slur in *C* and *C'/D/E*—this should have been deleted with the revision of m. 198 in *C*.

M. 204, staves 1 and 2, beat 2, the articulations conform to analogous m. 45. Mm. 209 and 210, staff 1, the caesuras conform to analogous mm. 50 and 51 (see report for m. 50). M. 215, staff 1, beat 1, lower voice, the d'-natural/f'[-sharp] dyad is preceded by only an eighth rest—an error. M. 220, staff 3, note 2 has no staccato dot in *E*—faded from pressing.

II

Widor's abundantly inventive muse is manifested here in some of his most graceful music for organ. An orchestral quality is apparent in the pizzicato effect of the double pedal, scored in the manner of divisi cellos and double basses, and in the variety of somewhat stringlike accompanimental figurations. The renowned French cellist Jules Delsart heard this music in terms of his own instrument and transcribed it for cello and piano; other arrangements were made for violin and piano (titled "Romance pathétique") and viola and piano.

The formal structure of the movement is A B A'. A smoothly flowing arpeggiated accompaniment in the A section yields to a more rhythmically animated arpeggiated figuration in the B section, where the melodic interest is based on the opening phrase of the A section. The central section melds seamlessly into the reprise with yet a third, gently undulating, accompanimental treatment. Widor made two small corrections in this movement, reported below. Edition *E* is the principal source.

Edition *B* differs from all subsequent editions in m. 70, staff 2, beat 1, where dyad 1 is e'/d"-flat, dyad 2 is b'-natural/e", dyad 3 is e'/d"[-flat]—errors; the engraver obviously read the upper note of dyads 1 and 3 and the whole of dyad 2 a third too high. In editions *B* and *B'*, m. 9, staff 2, beat 4, note 3 has no sharp.

Performance Insight

A rule that needs to be observed in Widor's works, as well as those growing out of the nineteenth-century French school in general, is worth repeating here.

Two voices following one another on the same note must be tied [as in ex. 2a]:

Example 2a

It is impossible to detach the g' from e" in the soprano without misleading the listener, who would suppose the text to be conceived [as in ex. 2b]:

Example 2b

The movement of one of the voices running into a neighboring voice does not take any of the value from it, [as in ex. 3a]:

Example 3a

The e" of the soprano must preserve its duration and that of the alto merge with the sustained note, otherwise . . . the effect produced [would be as in ex. 3b]:

Example 3b

and the listener would again be misled.*

There are several places in the present movement where common-note ties are required. For instance, in m. 18, staff 1, tie the e' notes under the second slur. In m. 42, staff 1, beat 3, do not break the d' whole note when the soprano merges with it.

Critical Notes

Mm. 15–18, staff 1, lower voice, slurs follow those of analogous mm. 32–35, staff 2. M. 16, staff 1, beat 2, lower voice, an arrow points to note (b') in all editions—this is the sole use of such an indication in the organ symphonies; Widor appears to be drawing the performer's attention to the sequential repetition of the four-note phrase commencing at m. 15, beat 2 (see slurring in analogous mm. 32–33 and 84–85, staff 2, lower voice); the problem is that rearticulating b' would mean breaking the upper voice slur and ignoring the policy of tied common notes. M. 21, staff 2, lower voice, note 1 has no dot in any edition—an error. Mm. 31–35, staff 2, upper voice, slurs follow those of analogous mm. 14–18, staff 1. M. 35, staff 1, beat 4, lower-voice tie to m. 36 follows that of analogous m. 37.

M. 71, it seems to the editor that *a tempo* should read "Tempo I." M. 74, staff 2, a continuous slur follows that for all other statements of this phrase. M. 78, staff 1, beat 4, dyad 2, *Riem 8* has natural on a'—this is certainly a slip of the hand where a'-sharp is clearly the correct member of this dominant-seventh harmony, and the sharp follows analogous m. 9 (where the sharp is lacking from a' until edition *C'*). M. 83, staff 1, upper voice, note 2, the slur to m. 84 follows that of analogous m. 31. Mm. 83–87, staff 2, upper voice, slurs follow those of analogous mm. 14–18, staff 1. M. 90, staff 1, upper voice, note 1, the omission of the incoming tie was an engraver's error made (as usual) at a change of system. M. 98, a double barline for the coda seems an appropriate structural demarcation, given those of mm. 2, 40, and 72.

---

*Charles-Marie Widor, preface to *Jean-Sébastien Bach: Oeuvres complètes pour orgue*, 1 (New York: G. Schirmer, 1914), viii. Italics in the original distinguish rules from explications of rules.

III

This movement functions in the symphony as a scherzo, but not the elfin type found in Symphonie IV; here the music has an aura of the sinister, twitching and turning without cease. The crisply articulated phrases in very rapid tempo lend a certain brusqueness, but what could become pure bravura is given musical worth by frequent use of canonic imitation. There are no formal dividing lines, yet the ternary structure is easily discernible with the introduction of a new theme at measure 92 and the return of the main theme at measure 162. As usual, Widor infuses his reprise with fresh ideas. Unrelenting pedal points in the form of trills, a hint of the B theme, and a shift of the canonically imitative voice from left hand to pedal add elements of variation.

There are two versions of the movement: *B/B'* and *C/C'/D/E*. These are identical until measure 230. Appendix 2 gives the ending of version *B/B'*. For the final version, edition *E* is the principal source.

CRITICAL NOTES

M. 24, staff 1, dyad 1, despite tenuto in all editions, this might be played staccato, following similar m. 32 as well as the canonic imitation of the phrase (m. 25, staff 2, dyad 1). M. 33, staff 3, the editor suggests coupling **G** to Pédale with the commencement of the Pédale's melodic phrase and in coincidence with the manual's **GPR**; Widor indicates "Péd. **PR**" at m. 45, which seems to indicate that the Pédale be increased earlier.

M. 59, staff 2, lower voice, note 1 (a quarter) is stemmed with upper-voice eighth note in *E*—an engraver's error made when attempting to improve the deteriorating plates. M. 83, staff 3, note 1, staccato added by analogy with m. 79. M. 87, staff 2, note 1, staccato added by analogy with m. 79. M. 90, staff 3, note 3, staccato added by analogy with m. 82. M. 91, staves 2 and 3, note 1, staccato added by analogy with m. 83.

Mm. 142–90, "Anches Récit" is the only registrational directive given, though m. 191 specifies "GP Fonds," implying the introduction of the Positif and Grand-orgue Anches somewhere in this passage; the *ff* in m. 152 would be an appropriate place to add the Positif Anches; although a *fff* dynamic mark—Widor's usual sign for introducing the **G** Anches—is lacking, if the performer opts to add the Grand-orgue Anches, the editor suggests either m. 161, the upbeat eighth note, or m. 180, the second half of beat 2, as possible options.

M. 226, staff 1, upper voice, the omission of the incoming tie was an engraver's error made (as usual) at a change of system; staff 3, note 1 has no staccato dot—an error made when the revised ending was engraved. M. 227, staff 1, natural is on b″ instead of c‴—an error made when the revised ending was engraved. M. 232, staff 1, second half of beat 1, sharp is on g″ instead of a″ in *C/C'/D/E*—an error made when reengraving the revised ending; edition corrected by analogy with m. 224 and *B/B'* (see Appendix 2, m. 232). M. 242, staff 1, upper voice, note 2 has no eighth flag—an error.

IV. Variations

A Prélude, given as Appendix 3, precedes this movement in editions *B* and *B'*, where it serves as an elaborate exposition of the theme of the Variations. Opening with the theme stated in the manner of a ground bass, the variations proceed like a baroque passacaglia, rather than the usual theme and variations suggested by the title. An important parallel can be drawn between Widor's use of this baroque variation form and Brahms' employment of it in his exactly contemporaneous Symphony No. 4, fourth movement. Widor, like Brahms, was very much attracted to the musical past, especially Bach, and, like Brahms, revived old forms at a time when novel musical structures were being sought. This movement, however, is not as strict in its adherence to passacaglia procedures as Widor's baroque models or even the Brahms example, where one variation follows another directly. Embracing a broad range of expressive moods, some of the variations are linked by interludes and transitions. But even when the theme has moved out of the foreground, fragments and other suggestions of it remain to bind the sections together in an effective manner.

Deeply rooted in classical traditions, Widor still shows himself to be a composer of his own time as he wields the musical language of the late nineteenth century. The theme comprises two symmetrical phrases, the second a major third lower than the first and altered in its ending. In the variations that follow, the variety of styles, rhythmic ideas, and elaborative counterpoint reflect Widor in his most serious mood. He utilizes the organ as deftly as an orchestra. The two great climactic buildups and ensuing denouments are reminiscent of Bruckner. Widor demands the utmost from both performer and listener, but the rewards are ample. In terms of sheer workmanship, this may be the greatest movement of the symphonies.

There are two almost identical versions: *B/B'* and *C/C'/D/E*. For the final version, edition *E* is the principal source.

The form of the Variations may be outlined as follows. Measures 1–8: theme; measures 8–13: link; measures 14–21: first entry; measures 22–29: second entry; measures 30–32: link; measures 33–36: third entry, incomplete; measures 37–44: fourth entry; measures 45–52: link; measures 53–60: fifth entry; measures 61–66: link; measures 67–72: sixth entry in free style; measures 73–87: cadenzalike interlude; measures 88–98: seventh entry plus extension; measures 98–117: interlude (coda material); measures 118–125: eighth entry, two statements of first phrase; measures 126–133: ninth entry, two free statements of first phrase; measures 134–151: extension in the form of an interlude; measures 152–156: anticipation of tenth entry; measures 157–164: tenth entry, two statements of first phrase; measures 165–179: interlude with thematic fragments;

measures 180–190: eleventh entry plus extension; measures 190–211: coda plus Adagio.

Version *B/B'* differs from version *C/C'/D/E* as follows. M. 30, staff 3, note 3 is F. M. 84, staff 2, beat 2 is f, b[-flat] (with *fff* dynamic mark), a-flat, g-flat sixteenth notes beamed to g[-flat] (tied from previous note), f, d'-flat sixteenth notes grouped as a triplet. M. 87, staff 3, beat 1 is at rest; beat 2 is sixteenth rest, f', f, g sixteenth notes beamed to g (tied from previous note), g-sharp, a sixteenth notes grouped as a triplet. M. 88, staff 3, beat 1, note 1 is A; beat 2 is c-sharp, e, d, c[-sharp], B[-flat], A sixteenth notes. M. 89, staff 3, beat 1, note 1 is G; beat 2 is E, F, G sixteenth notes grouped as a triplet beamed to D, C-sharp sixteenth notes, C-natural eighth note tied into next measure. Mm. 91–98, staff 3 is in octaves. M. 92, staff 2, chord 2 includes e'. M. 95, staff 3, notes 4 and 5 are dotted eighth note, sixteenth note. M. 98, staff 3, upper voice is d dotted quarter note, quarter rest, eighth rest. M. 104, staff 2, note 4 has no trill—probably an error since analogous m. 196 includes it.

CRITICAL NOTES

M. 15, staff 2 has no change to treble clef at beat 2—an error; instead, the clef is given at the end of m. 17 (the correct placement is marked in *Riem* 8). M. 33, staff 1, beat 2, lower voice, the editor feels that note 5 should be g'-natural, but no such correction is marked in *Emend* 1, *Emend* 2, *Riem* 8, or *Schw* 7–8.

M. 53, staff 1, b"-natural upper auxiliary is confirmed in *Riem* 8. Mm. 61–72, triplet groupings are indicated, if at all, variously with numerals alone, numerals with triplet slurs, and triplet slurs without numerals—edition provides indications for one measure as a model at each pattern change. M. 70, staff 2, beat 1 has an eighth rest after the eighth-note dyad—an error—followed by another eighth rest instead of the editorial sixteenth rest—another error. M. 72, staff 2, triplet slurs without numerals appear over each pair of notes following a sixteenth rest. M. 83, staff 2, the editor feels that note 8 should be c"-natural, but no such correction is marked in *Emend* 1, *Emend* 2, *Riem* 8, or *Schw* 7–8. M. 93, staff 2, chord 1, lowest note has no dot—an error. M. 98, staff 3, beat 2 has superfluous rests in *C/C'/D/E*—these should have been deleted after the revision from *B/B'*.

M. 106, staff 2, beat 2, note 2, the natural follows analogous m. 198 and *Riem* 8. M. 125, staff 2, last note has superfluous tie in all editions. M. 138, staff 2, note 3 is c" in all editions—edition follows analogous m. 137.

Mm. 157–58, staff 2, although the upstemmed e eighth notes should be stemmed separately and dotted to be metrically correct, Widor's orthographic practice in this situation is to let the tie compensate for the notational inaccuracy. M. 159, staff 2, e dotted eighth note is stemmed with e sixteenth note and has no dot—separating stemming and dotted value follow the intention of analogous mm. 157–58 (see report there).

M. 168, staff 2, beat 2, upper voice, note has no dot in any edition—an error. M. 170, staff 3, note has no incoming tie—the engraver neglected to continue the tie from m. 169 (on the previous system in the source). M. 179, staves 1 and 2, beat 2, note 5 has *fff* concurrently with the *fff* (Pédale Anches) of staff 3 in all editions; this dynamic mark for the manuals seems premature and conflicts with the crescendo hairpin leading to the *fff* at m. 180, note 1. M. 180, staff 3 has a redundant *fff* concurrently with *fff* (Grand-orgue Anches) of staves 1 and 2 in all editions. M. 188, staff 1, upper voice, note 2 as no eighth flag in any edition —an error.

V. Adagio

In Widor's organ music, perhaps nowhere in his conception more broadly orchestral; yet this movement never ceases to be music of the organ. The mood is set by a quasi-Wagnerian, chromatically inflected opening gesture that could easily be realized by the cello section of an orchestra. The subsequent long-breathed main theme, one of the composer's most eloquent, is constructed of wide, expressive leaps, and compact chromatic turns. Singing first in the middle register of his organ/orchestra, the main theme is surrounded in a tapestry of accompanimental counterpoint drawn from the theme itself. The theme reappears in the upper register in an extended form. The B section of this A B A' structure is a fugato with a subject of particularly salient rhythmic character and distinctive phrasing. As it develops, the A theme is brought back as countermelody, and the fugato style finally dissolves into an arpeggiated accompaniment that ushers back the A' section. The motion abruptly comes to a close with the quiet chords of the coda.

A minuscule difference between edition *B* and subsequent editions (all identical) occurs in measures 110–13, staff 2, where the lower voice is c[-sharp]. Edition *E* is the principal source.

CRITICAL NOTES

M. 5, beat 2, in addition to the tie to m. 6 (e[-sharp] dotted half note) there is a slur to m. 7, beat 1 (e[-sharp] eighth note)—this is likely an engraver's error; the slur should have been a tie from m. 6, e[-sharp] dotted half note. M. 12, staff 1, although the melodic phrases are usually slurred from the anacrusis note (cf. mm. 8, 10, 18, 20, directly analogous 22, and 26), here and in analogous m. 92, the phrasing seems to begin intentionally with the downbeat. M. 21, staff 2, beat 3, upper-voice tie to m. 22 added by analogy with m. 11. Mm. 33–64, Widor is somewhat laconic in marking the phrasing and articulation in the B section (especially after the fugal exposition, ending at m. 41), and the editor has chosen not to inflict upon the text scores of bracketed articulations when it is clear by analogy how they should be played throughout. M. 48, staff 2, notes 2 and 3, the slur fades progressively from editions after *B'*.

M. 71, staff 1, note 1 has **P** through edition *C*;—it appears that this manual directive simply faded from later pressings, rather than having been intentionally deleted, in which case **G** should have been inserted.

VI. Finale

Even Widor's most ardent admirers and disciples were not always unanimous in their praise of his work. Albert Schweitzer betrayed his feelings about this movement when he wrote in his score (now *Schw* 7–8) across the top of the Finale: "Wie schade dass Widor das geschriebe [sic] hat!" (What a shame that Widor wrote this!). Albert Riemenschneider, on the other hand, referred to it as "a movement of almost barbaric splendor and exuberance. . . . It rushes on with irresistible sway and shows the Master in one of his finest rhythmic moods."*

A full rondo, A B A C A B A, this is not of the Haydnesque, playful, lighthearted variety. Characterized by insistent rhythm, angular leaps, and strong-beat appoggiaturas, the austere main theme, with its spare, sharp staccato accompaniment, immediately presents the listener with music of imposing power and gravity. A series of syncopations serves to halt the momentum and round off the A section with a full cadence (m. 36). A secondary idea over an arpeggiated figuration forms the contrasting B section. This yields to a connective passage (m. 77), using A-theme motives, that leads to the second A section (m. 100). The central C section (m. 144) moves through several keys and utilizes A-theme motives in a texture requiring one hand to play on two manuals at once. A climactic full reprise of the A theme follows (m. 182). The arpeggiated figuration of the B section returns (m. 215), but this time it accompanies the A-theme motive with no recurrence of the B theme itself. Another connective passage (m. 237), again using A-theme motives, leads to a shortened reprise for the fourth A section.

There are two versions of the Finale, identical—except for two octave transpositions—until the last eight measures: B and B'/C/C'/D/E. Widor must have realized that something altogether extraordinary was needed to conclude this symphony, and the ending in the first edition did not fulfill that need. For edition B' he devised a final cadence of harmonically striking character. The ending of edition B is given as Appendix 4. For the final version, edition E is the principal source.

Critical Notes

The registration directive includes "Tous le [sic] Claviers et la Pédale accouplés au Grand-orgue" in all editions; consequently, the full **GPR** directive is given in two measures (mm. 151 and 159, staff 3) where Widor uses the abbreviated **G**. M. 64, staff 2, half note has no stem in *E*—faded from pressing.

M. 208, staff 2, second half of beat 2, the two upper notes are stemmed together—an error; edition follows

---

*Albert Riemenschneider, "Program Notes on the Widor 'Symphonies,'" *The American Organist* 8, no. 7 (July 1925): 268.

analogous m. 29. M. 250, staff 2, beat 2, upper voice has eighth rest, then merges with lower voice. M. 264, staff 2, dyad 2, natural follows descending chromatic pattern and is supported by *Riem* 8.

Appendix 1

[I] Editions *B* and *B'*, mm. 34–40, 52–56, 68–85, 135–38, 146–52, 168–85, 215–20. To perform either edition complete, play mm. 1–33 of edition *E*, noting the variants reported below; then mm. 34–40 in this Appendix (mm. 34 and 39 in *E* equal mm. 34 and 40 in this Appendix); then mm. 40–50 of *E*; then mm. 52–56 in this Appendix (mm. 51 and 55 in *E* equal mm. 52 and 56 in this Appendix); then mm. 56–66 of *E*, noting the variant reported below; then mm. 68–85 in this Appendix (mm. 67 and 84 in *E* equal mm. 68 and 85 in this Appendix); then mm. 85–133 of *E*, noting the variants reported below; then mm. 135–38 in this Appendix (mm. 134 and 137 in *E* equal mm. 135 and 138 in this Appendix); then mm. 138–44 of *E*, noting the variants reported below; then mm. 146–52 in this Appendix (mm. 145 and 149 in *E* equal mm. 146 and 152 in this Appendix); then mm. 150–64 of *E*; then mm. 168–85 in this Appendix (mm. 165 and 183 in *E* equal mm. 168 and 185 in this Appendix); then mm. 184–212 of *E*, noting the variants reported below; then mm. 215–20 in this Appendix (mm. 213 and 218 in *E* equal mm. 215 and 220 in this Appendix); then mm. 219–38 of *E*.

Aside from the *Emend* 1 revisions that were never used, as given in the commentary to the first movement, *Emend* 1 contains some revisions that seem more relevant to *B'* than *C* because the passage was further revised for *C*. For the purpose of examining the editions of this Appendix, the editor has selected those emendations which might be considered more as corrections applicable to *B'* than as revisions planned for *C* (the measure numbers refer to the Appendix excerpts). M. 84, staff 1, lower voice, note 2 is eighth note followed by c"-natural eighth note. M. 137, staff 3, lower voice, note 2 is quarter note. M. 150, staff 2 has **G** after downbeat chord, and there is a slur and crescendo hairpin extending to the end of m. 151, where notes 4 and 5 are slurred. M. 182, staff 1, beat 1, upper voice is c'''[-sharp] quarter note, d'''[-sharp] eighth note; staff 2, beat 1, lower voice is b (tied from m. 181), a[-sharp], a-natural eighth notes.

Editions *B* and *B'* differ from edition *E* in mm. 1–33 as follows. The Récit registration is "Fonds et Anches 4, 8, 16." M. 9, staves 1 and 2, beat 2 has no **PR** directive.

Editions *B* and *B'* differ from edition *E* in mm. 56–66 as follows (measure number is for *E*; to obtain measure number for *B* and *B'*, add 1). M. 59, staff 1, note 7 is d"[-double sharp]—an error—it probably should be d"-sharp; staff 2, note 10 is d'[-sharp].

Editions *B* and *B'* differ from edition *E* in mm. 85–133 as follows (measure numbers are for *E*; to obtain measure numbers for *B* and *B'*, add 1). M. 85, staff 3, note is staccato (curiously, the analogous note in m. 89 has no staccato dot). M. 92, staff 2 has **GPR** directive. M. 98, staff 1, beat 2, note 1 has no double sharp; staff 2, note 1 is a-natural, note 3 is g[-sharp]; staff 3, beat 1 is d-sharp quarter note, d'[-sharp] eighth note slurred from m. 97 (Widor marked note 2 as c'[-sharp] in *Emend* 1), beat 2 is at rest. M. 99, staff 3 is at rest. M. 99–101, staves 1 and 2, g' and g" notes have no double sharp. M. 114, staff 1, beat 2 is f"[-sharp]/f'"[-sharp] dotted eighth notes beamed with g"-natural/g'"-natural, f"[-sharp]/f'"[-sharp], e"[-sharp]/e'"[-sharp] sixteenth notes; staff 2, beat 2 is f'[-sharp] dotted eighth note beamed with g'-natural, f'[-sharp], e'[-sharp] sixteenth notes (a slur extends from beat-1 chord to downbeat of m. 115); there is no *allargando* directive. M. 115, staff 1, beat 1 is f"[-sharp]/f'"[-sharp] quarter notes, f'[-sharp]/f"[-sharp] eighth notes, with no fermata, tied to beat 2; staff 2, beat 1 is f'[-sharp] quarter note, f'[-sharp] eighth note, with no fermata, tied to beat 2. M. 124, staves 1 and 2 have no caesuras. Mm. 125–30, staff 2, all notes are staccato except those under slurs.

Editions *B* and *B'* differ from edition *E* in mm. 138–44 as follows. Mm. 137–42, staff 2, all notes are staccato except those under slurs.

Editions *B* and *B'* differ from edition *E* in mm. 184–212 as follows (measure numbers are for *E*; to obtain measure numbers for *B* and *B'*, add 2). M. 196, staff 3, note 2 has no natural. M. 197, staff 1, note 3 has no natural. M. 198, staff 1, beat 2 is tied e'"[-sharp] eighth note, f'"[-sharp] quarter note tied into m. 199 (there is no lower voice); staff 3 is A[-sharp] eighth note, A-natural quarter note, G[-sharp] dotted quarter note.

Appendix 2

III. Version B/B', mm. 229–49. To perform this version complete, play mm. 1–228 of edition *E*, noting the variants reported below; then this Appendix. Edition *B'* is the principal source.

The opening registration for the Pédale is "Basses de 8 et de 16." M. 56, staff 3 has no registration directive.

Appendix 3

IV. Prélude. Version B/B'. In editions *B* and *B'*, this movement serves as a sort of chorale prelude to the following Variations movement. For unknown reasons Widor deleted it with edition *C*. The upper voice announces the theme of the Variations in three phrases. Wrought in a beautiful polyphonic style that anticipates the Variations, each phrase is first presented in five-part counterpoint, played on all the foundations of the organ, and then quietly echoed in four-part counterpoint —sometimes embellished discreetly—in an antiphonal manner on the Récit. The quiet coda abandons the strict contrapuntal style as it intones the first phrase one more time. Ending on the dominant of the D-minor Variations, this relatively brief piece serves as a perfect introduction; the editor finds its deletion from the symphony particularly regrettable. No revisions were made to this movement. Edition *B'* is the principal source.

The registration directive calls for "tous les claviers accouplés au Grand-orgue." Therefore, **GPR** has been instated in the mānuals in lieu of the original **G** directive.

Appendix 4

VII. Finale. Edition B, mm. 261–69. To perform this edition complete, play mm. 1–260 of version *B'/C-/C'/D/E*, with the variants given below; then this Appendix.

M. 136, staff 1, beat 2, play the phrase beginning on **R** and continuing to m. 137, note 5, an octave higher. M. 137, staff 2, beat 1, play the phrase beginning on **R** and continuing to m. 138, note 1, an octave higher.

Widor's *Avant-propos*

Although it may not be customary to place a preface at the front of musical editions, I believe it is necessary to put one here in order to explain the character, the style, the procedures of registration, and the sign conventions of these eight symphonies.

Old instruments had almost no reed stops: two colors, white and black, foundation stops and mixture stops—that was their entire palette; moreover, each transition between this white and this black was abrupt and rough; the means of graduating the body of sound did not exist. Consequently, Bach and his contemporaries deemed it pointless to indicate registrations for their works—the mixture stops traditionally remaining appropriate to rapid movements, and the foundation stops to pieces of a more solemn pace.

The invention of the "swell box" dates back to just before the end of the eighteenth century. In a work published in 1772, the Dutchman Hess de Gouda expresses the admiration he felt upon hearing Handel, in London, coming to grips with the new device; some time later, in 1780, Abbé Vogler recommends the use of the "box" in the German manufacture of instruments. The idea gained ground, but without great artistic effect—for in spite of the most perspicacious efforts,* they did not succeed in going beyond the limits of a thirty-key manual and an insignificant number of registers.

It was necessary to wait until 1839 for the solution to the problem.

The honor for it redounds to French industry and the glory to Mr. A. Cavaillé-Coll. It is he who conceived the diverse wind pressures, the divided windchests, the pedal systems and the combination registers, he who applied for the first time Barker's pneumatic motors, created the family of harmonic stops, reformed and perfected the mechanics to such a point that each pipe—low or high, loud or soft—instantly obeys the touch of the finger, the keys becoming as light as those of a piano—the resistances being suppressed, rendering the combination of [all] the forces of the instrument practical. From this result: the possibility of confining an entire division in a sonorous prison—opened or closed at will—the freedom of mixing timbres, the means of intensifying them or gradually tempering them, the freedom of tempos, the sureness of attacks, the balance of contrasts, and, finally, a whole blossoming of wonderful colors—a rich palette of the most diverse shades: harmonic flutes, gambas, bassoons, English horns, trumpets, celestes, flue stops and reed stops of a quality and variety unknown before.

The modern organ is essentially symphonic. The new instrument requires a new language, an ideal other than scholastic polyphony. It is no longer the Bach of the fugue whom we invoke but the heartrending melodist, the preeminently expressive master of the Preludes, the Magnificat, the B-minor Mass, the cantatas, and the *St. Matthew Passion.*

But this "expressiveness" of the new instrument can only be subjective; it arises from mechanical means and cannot have spontaneity. While the stringed and wind instruments of the orchestra, the piano, and voices reign only by naturalness of accent and unexpectedness of attack, the organ, clothed in its primordial majesty, speaks as a philosopher: alone among all, it can put forth the same volume of sound indefinitely and thus inspire the religious idea of the infinite. Surprises and accents are not natural to it; they are lent to it, they are accents by adoption. It is clear that their use requires tact and discernment. It is also clear to what extent the organ symphony differs from the orchestral symphony. No confusion is to be feared. One will never write indiscriminately for the orchestra or for the organ, but henceforth one will have to exercise the same care with the combination of timbres in an organ composition as in an orchestral work.

Rhythm itself must come under the influence of modern trends: it must lend itself to a sort of elasticity of the measure, all the while preserving its rights. It must allow the musical phrase to punctuate its paragraphs and breathe when necessary, provided that it hold [the phrase] by the bit and that [the phrase] march to its step. Without rhythm, without this constant manifestation of the will returning periodically to the strong beat, the performer will not be listened to. How often the composer hesitates and abstains at the moment of writing on his score the *poco ritenuto* that he has in his thought! He does not dare, from fear that the exaggeration of the performer may weaken or break the flow of the piece. The indication is left out. We do not have the graphic means for emphasizing the end of a period, or reinforcing a chord by a type of pause of unnoticeable duration. Isn't it a great shame, especially since the organ is an instrument that draws all of its effect from time values?

As to terminology, the system indicating the disposition of timbres—usage having established nothing as yet—it seemed practical to me to note the manual and pedal registration at the head of each piece; to apportion by tone colors, rather than an exact nomenclature of stops, the intensity of the sonorities of the same family; to designate the manuals by their abbreviations (two or

---

*Experiments of Sébastien Erard: Organ constructed in 1826 for the chapel of the Legion of Honor at St.-Denis—Exposition at the Louvre in 1827.

more initials juxtaposed signifying the coupling of two or more manuals); to assume the reed stops always prepared; and finally to reserve fff for the full power of the organ, without having to mention the introduction of the ventil (Anches) pedals. In the combination **GR** [Grand-orgue, Récit], the crescendo applies only to the Récit, unless this crescendo leads to the fff, in which case all the forces of the instrument must enter little by little in order, flues and reeds.

It is unnecessary, I believe, to implore the same precision, the same coordination of the feet and hands in leaving a keyboard as in attacking it, and to protest against all carrying-over of the pedal after the time, an old-fashioned custom that has happily almost disappeared.

With the consummate musicians of today, the insufficiencies and shortcomings in musical notation become less worrisome; the composer is more certain of seeing his intentions understood and his implications perceived. Between him and the performer is a steadfast collaboration, which the growing number of virtuosos will render more intimate and fruitful every day.

Ch. M. W.

Symphonie VIII in B Major

Grand orgue: Fonds 16', 8', 4'
Positif: Fonds 8', 4'
Récit: Fonds 8', 4'; Anches 16', 8', 4'
Pédale: Basses 32', 16', 8', 4'

[I]

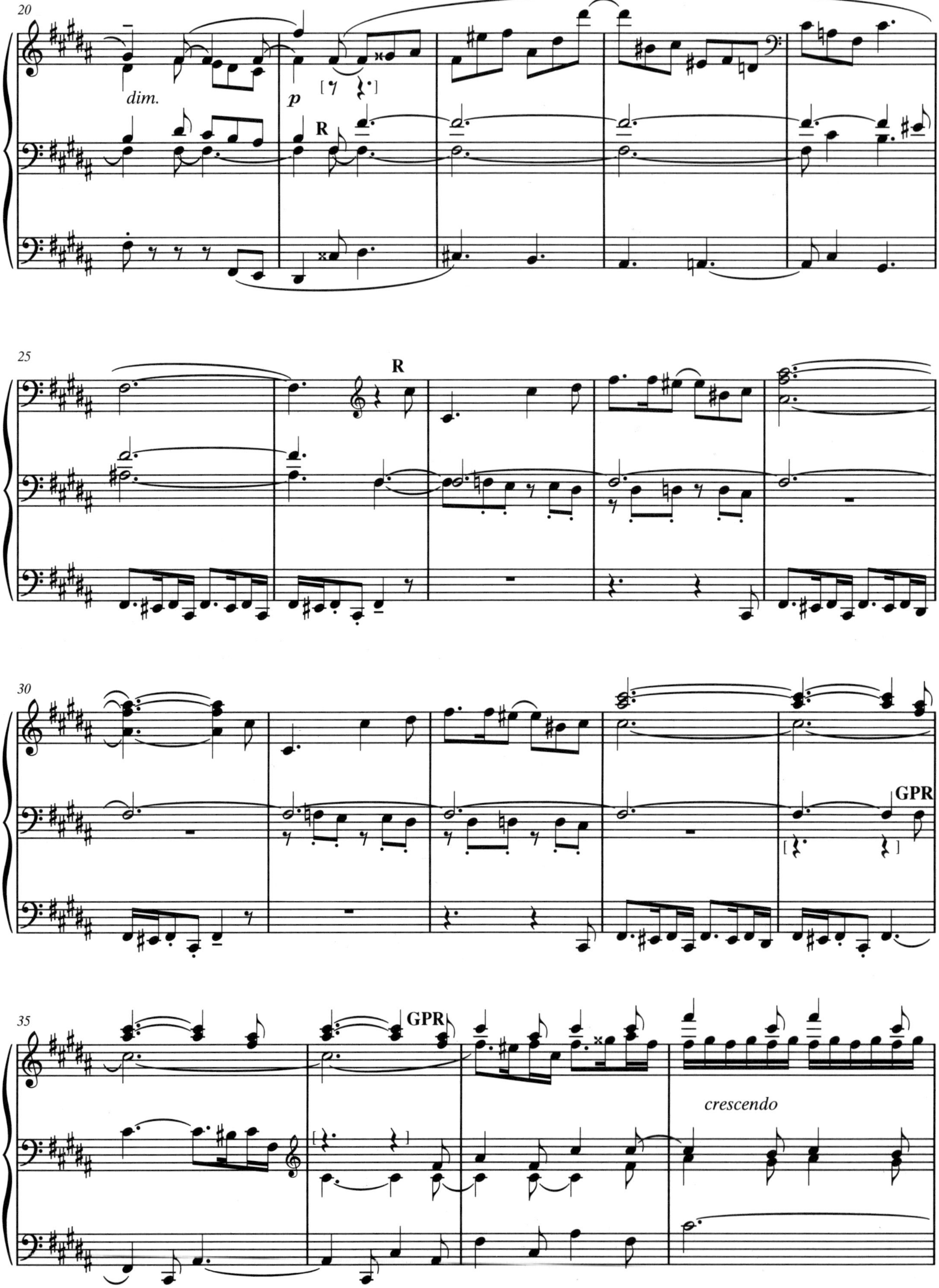
20
dim.
p
R
25
R
30
GPR
35
GPR
crescendo

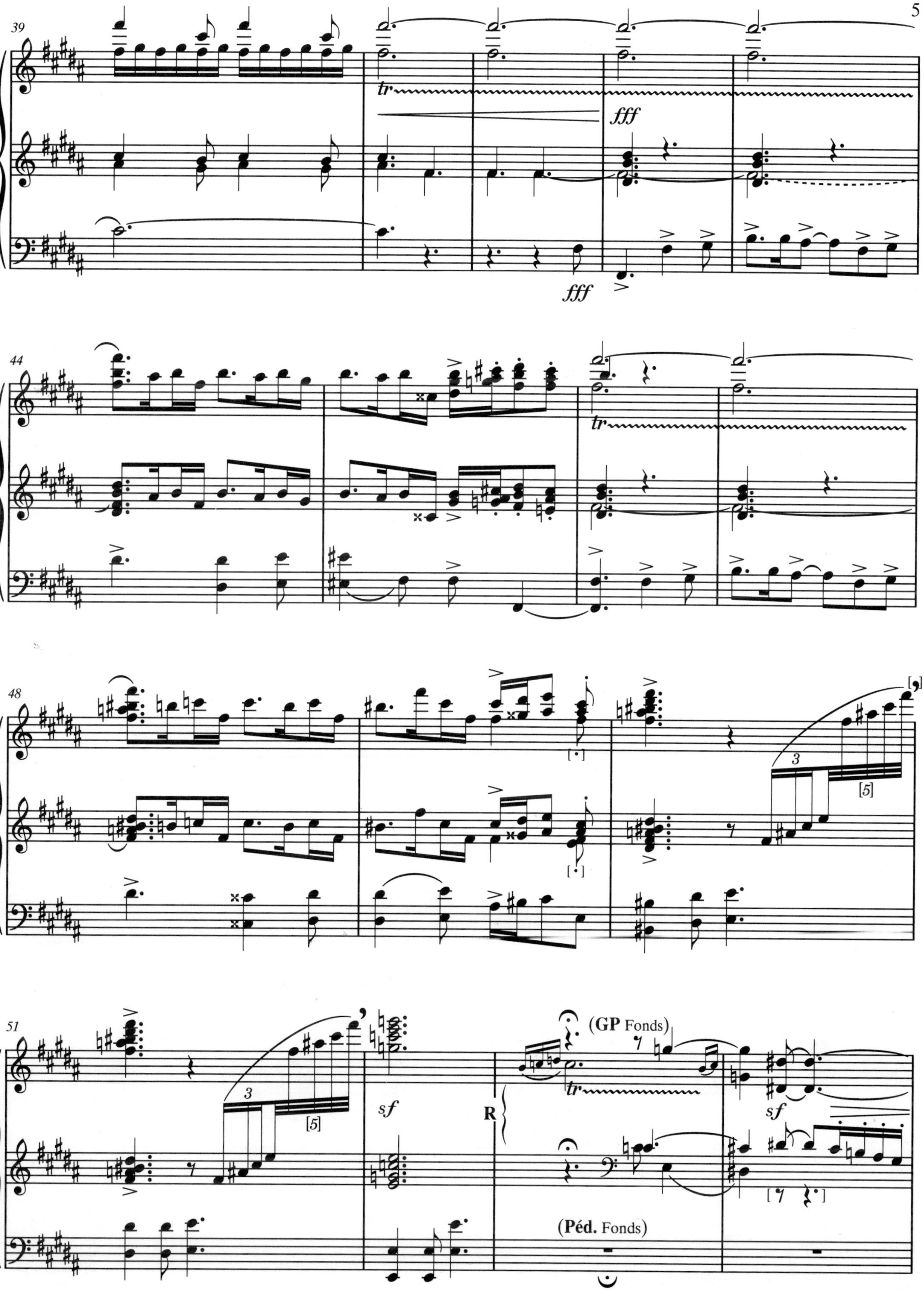
39
tr
fff
fff
44
tr
48
[5]
51
3
[5]
sf
R
(GP Fonds)
tr
sf
(Péd. Fonds)

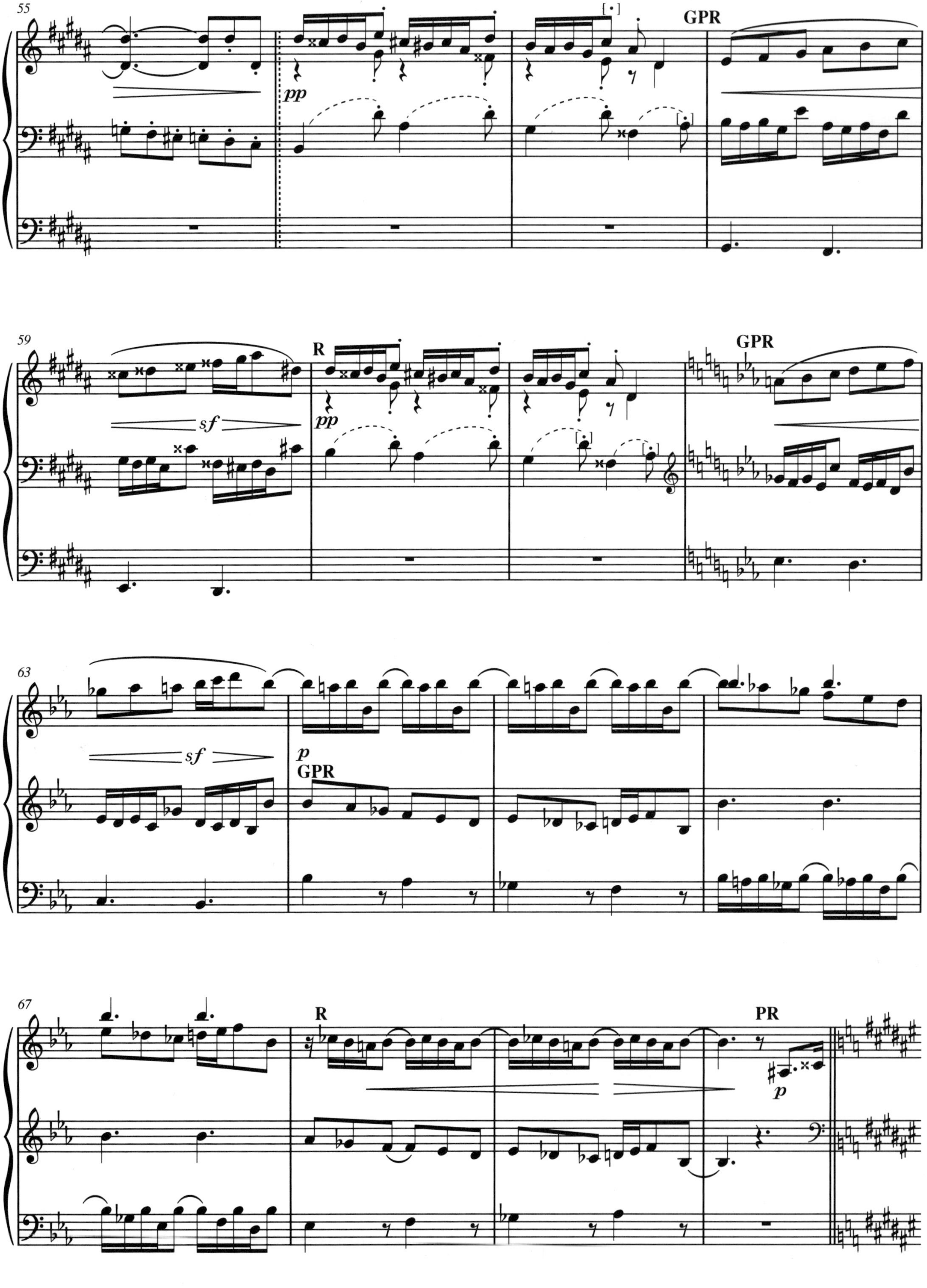
55
pp
GPR
59
R
sf
pp
GPR
63
sf
p
GPR
67
R
PR
p

71
GPR
R
76
Meno vivo
R Fonds
R
cresc.
PR
p
mf
80
Tempo I
R Anches
R
pp
85

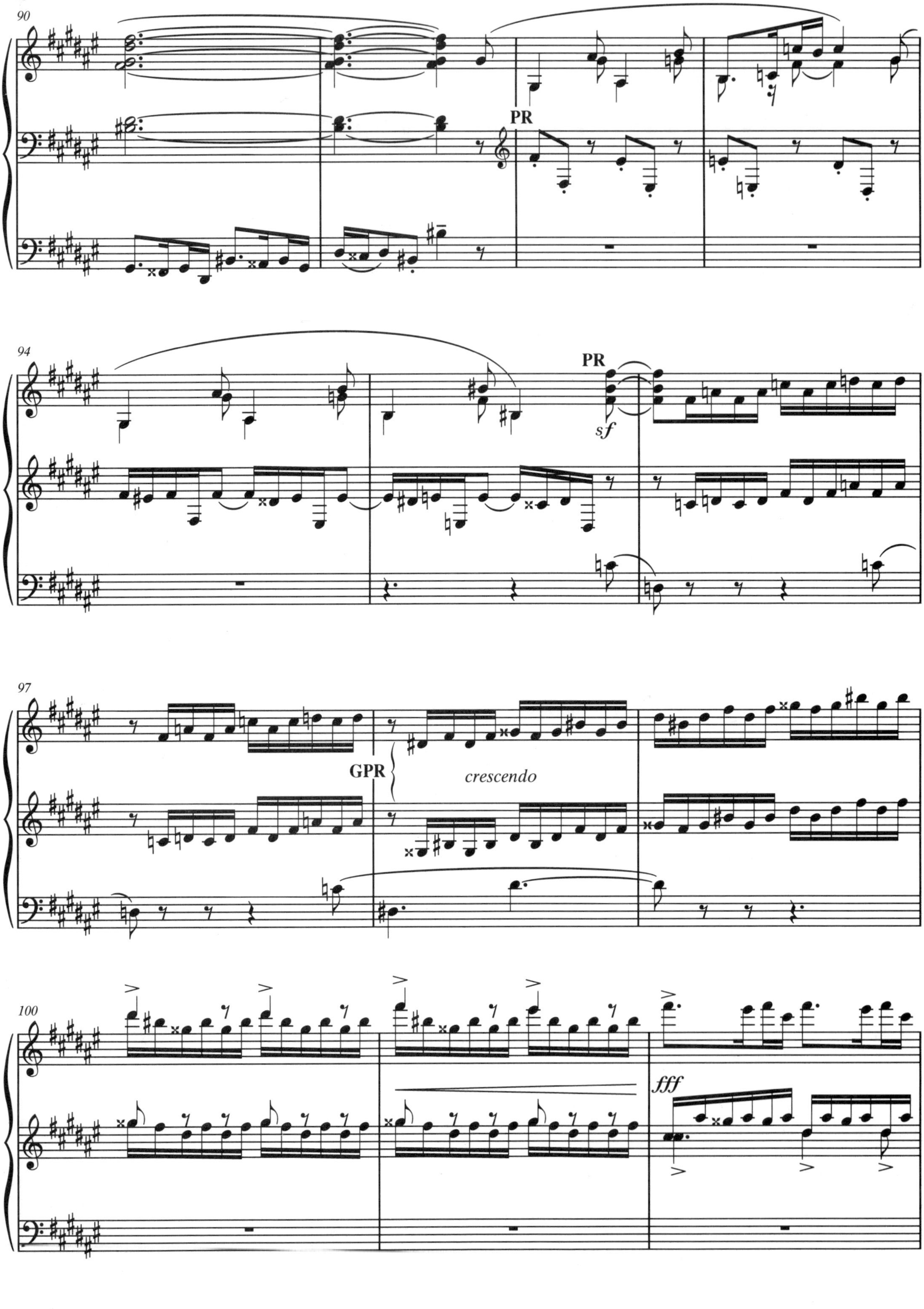
90
PR
94
PR
sf
97
GPR
crescendo
100
fff

103
fff
106
109
poco rit.
[a tempo]
sf
112
allargando
[a tempo]
(GP Fonds)
R
[𝄐] (Péd. Fonds)

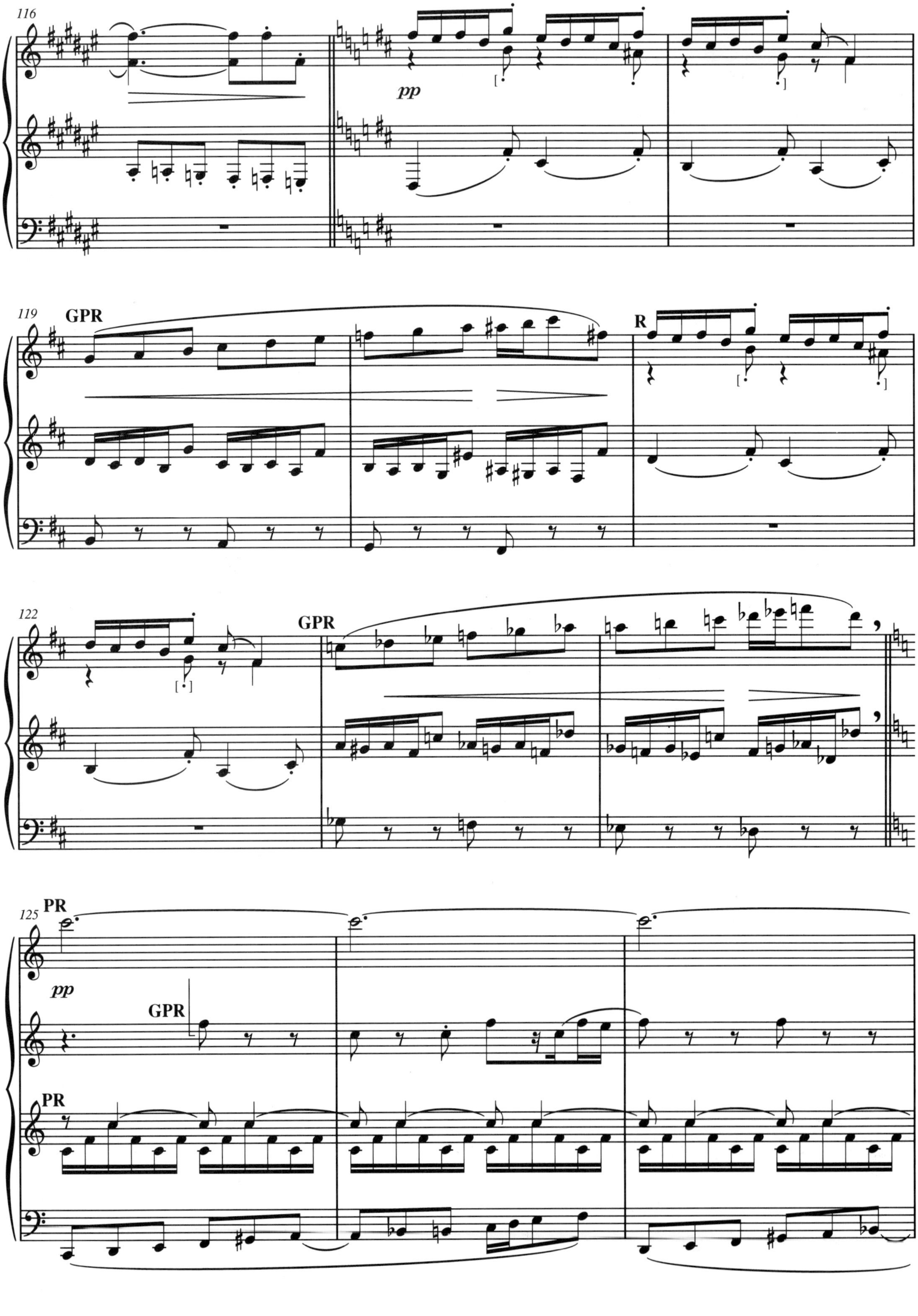
116
pp
119
GPR
R
122
GPR
125
PR
pp
GPR
PR

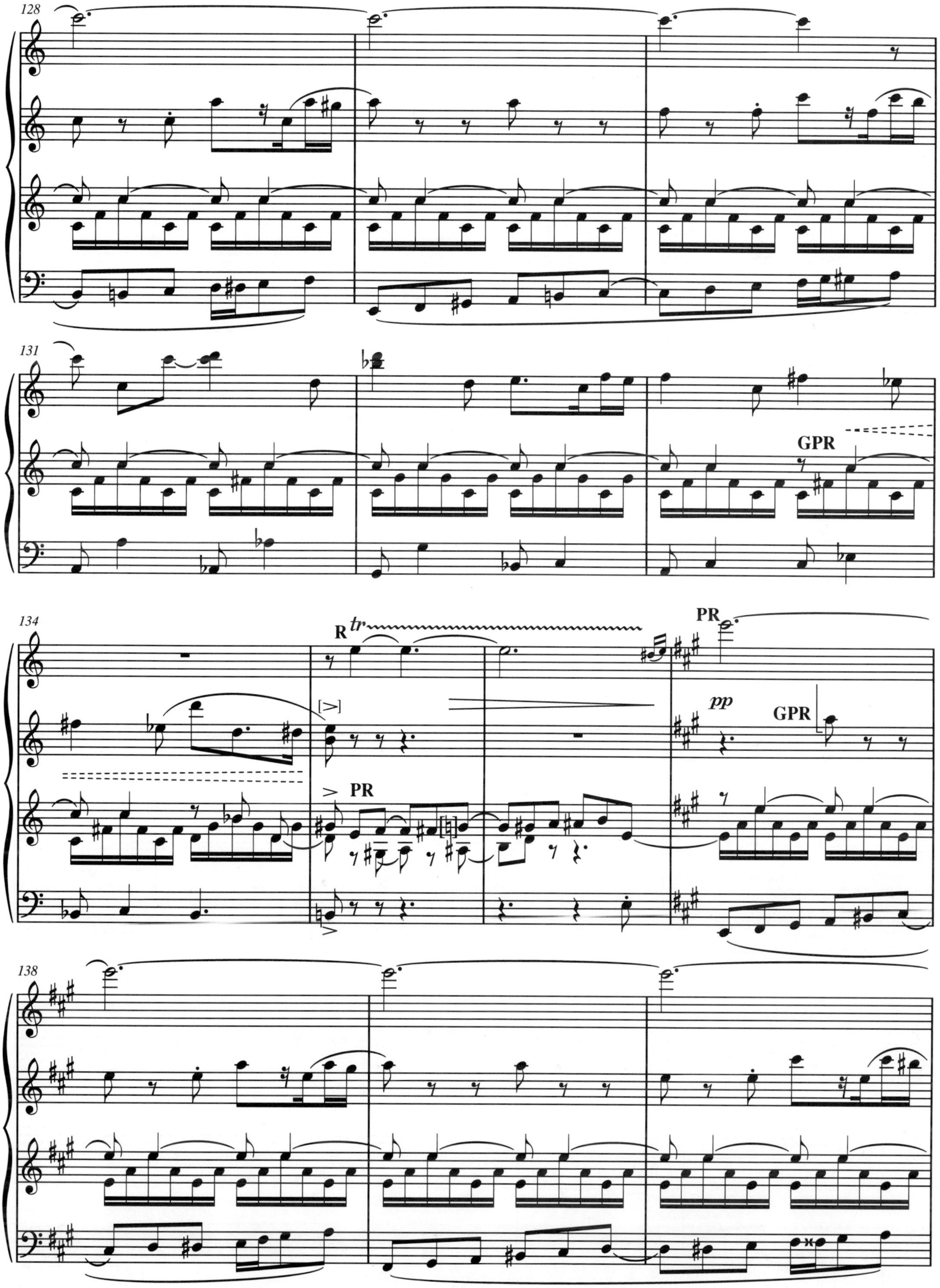
128
131
GPR
134
R
tr
PR
[>]
pp
GPR
PR
138

12

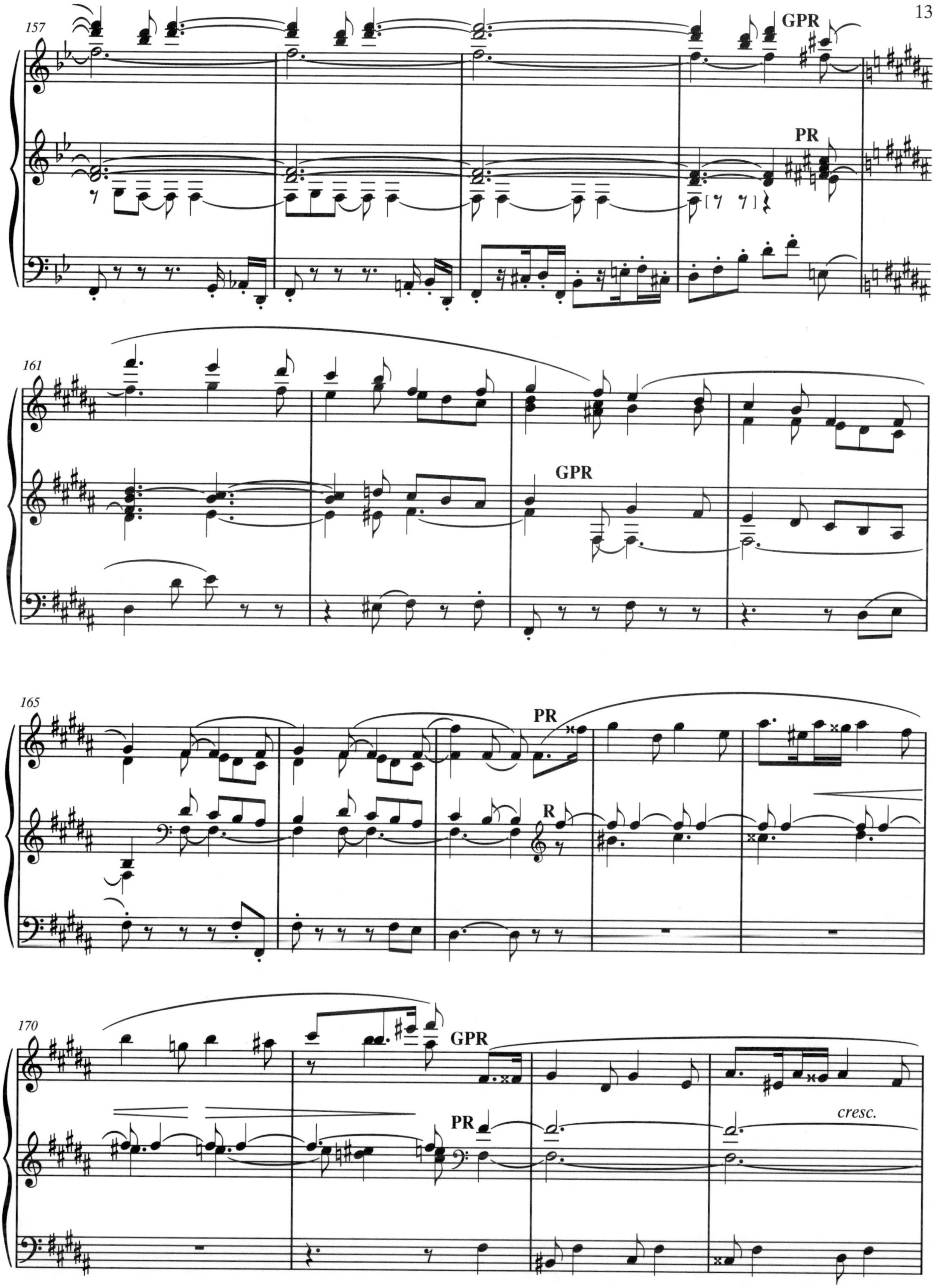
157
GPR
PR
161
GPR
165
PR
R
170
GPR
PR
cresc.

14

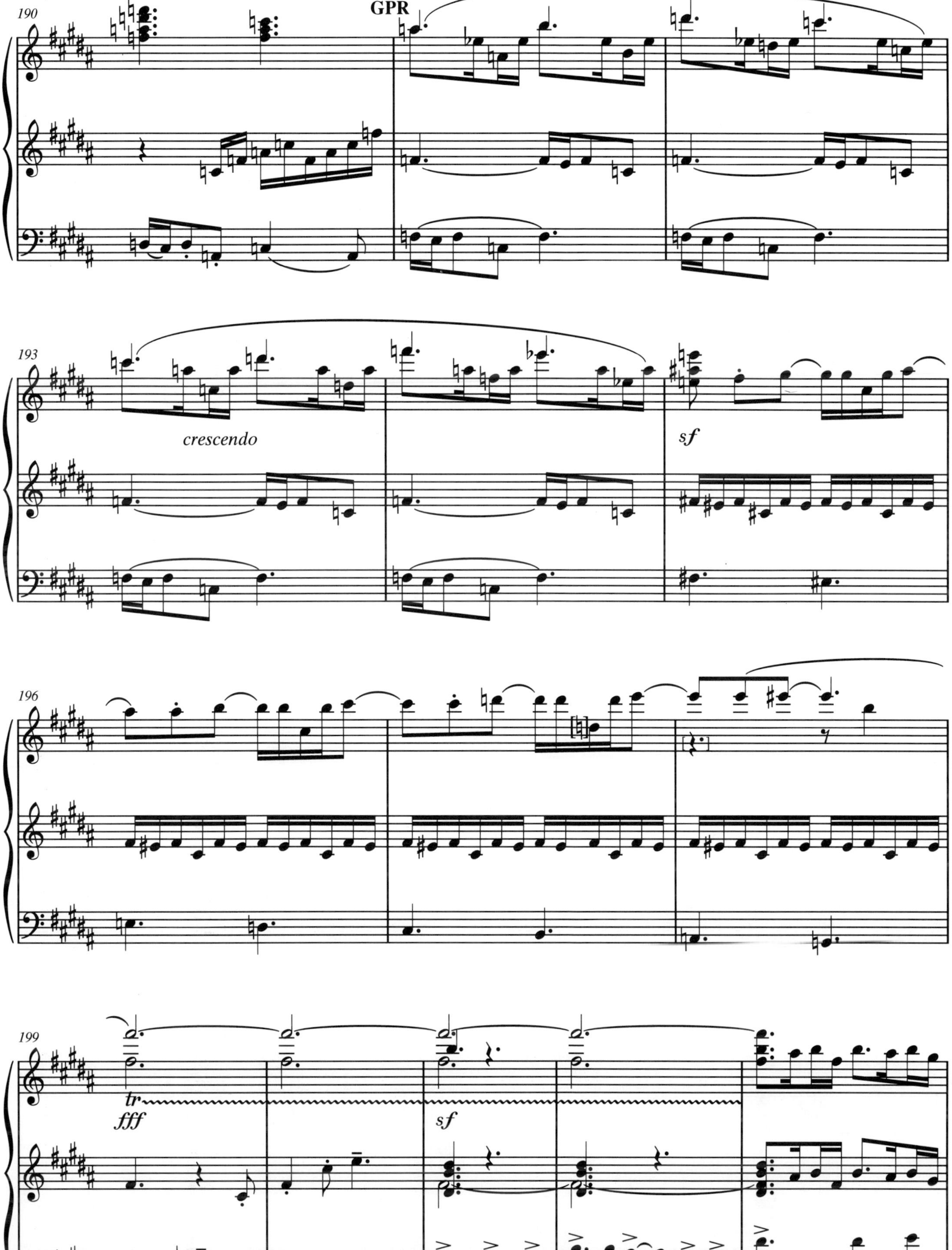
190
GPR
193
crescendo
sf
196
199
tr
fff
sf
fff

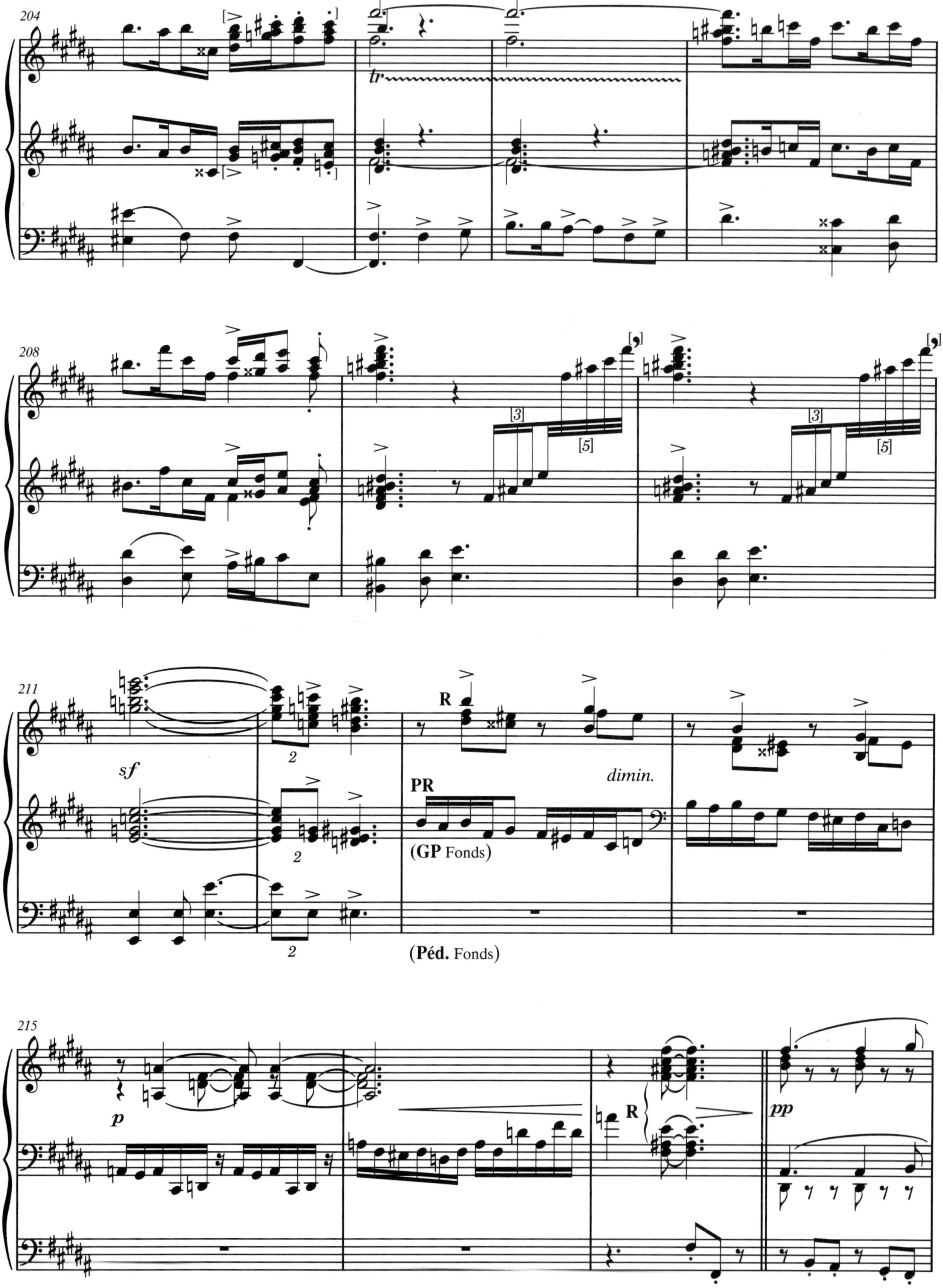
204
tr
208
[3]
[5]
211
sf
2
R
PR
(GP Fonds)
dimin.
(Péd. Fonds)
215
p
R
pp

17

Grand orgue: Flûte 8'
Positif: Flûtes 8', 4'
Récit: [Gambe 8',] Voix céleste
Pédale: Bourdons 16', 8'

II

Moderato cantabile ($\quarter = 70$)

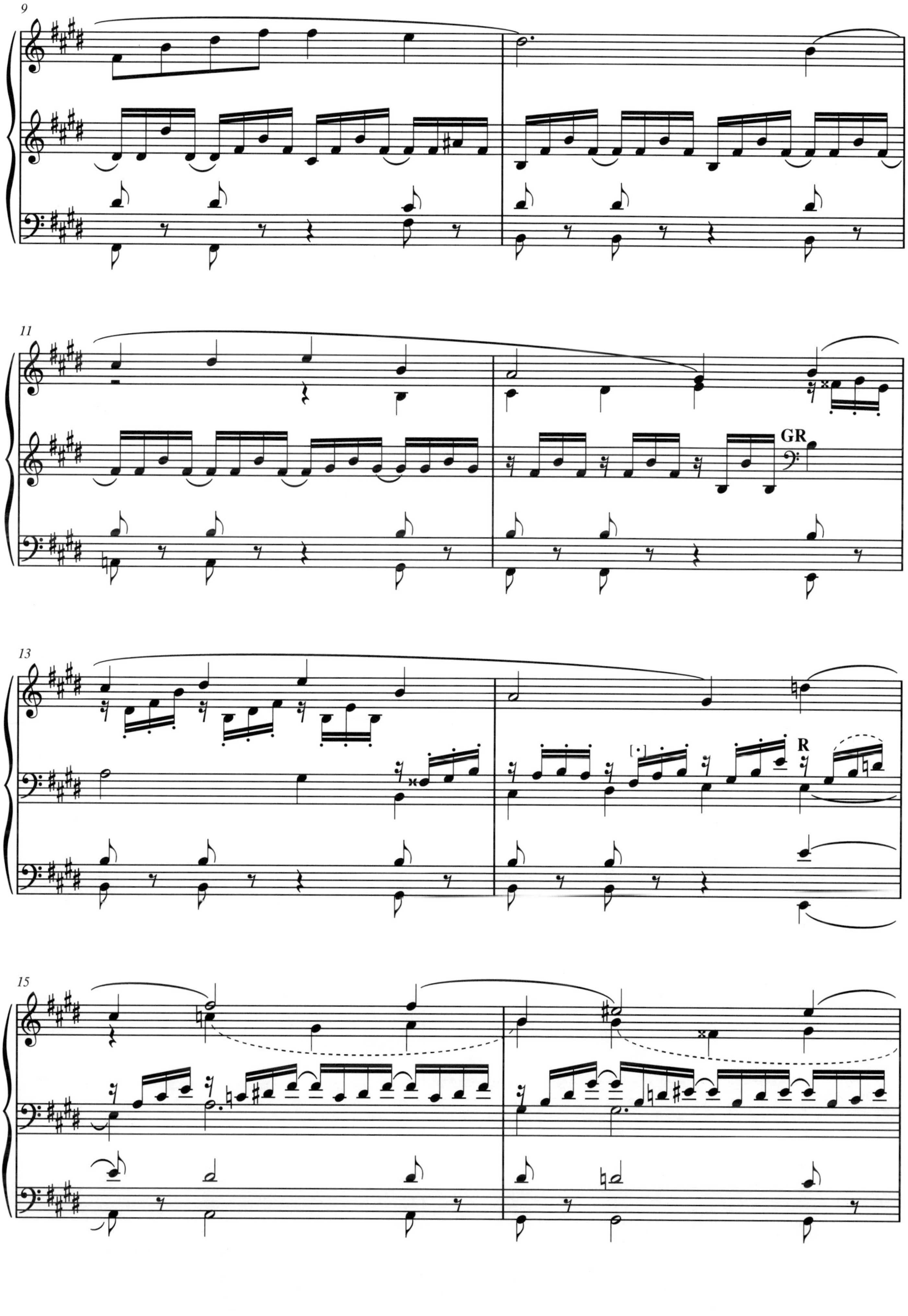
9
11
GR
13
R
15

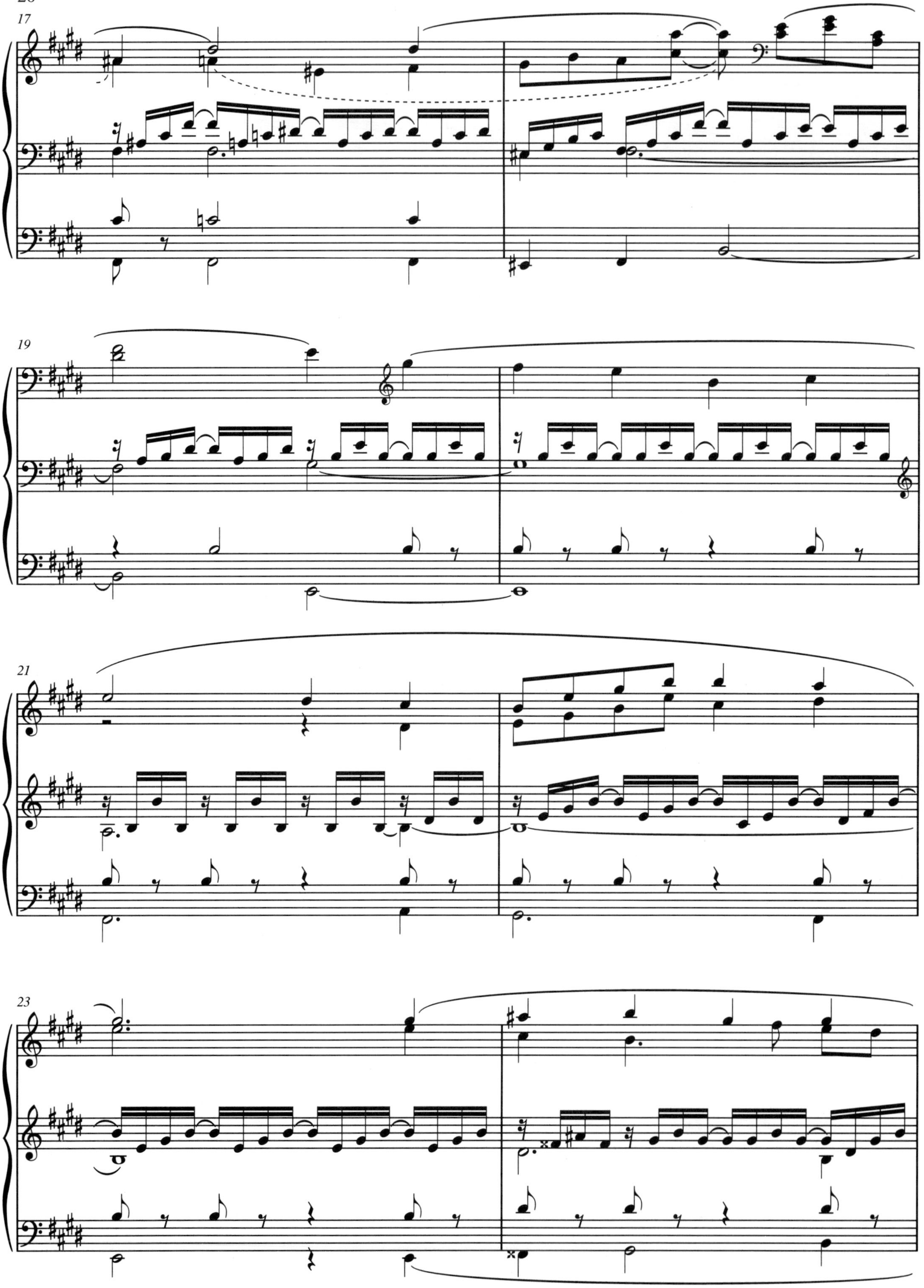
17
19
21
23

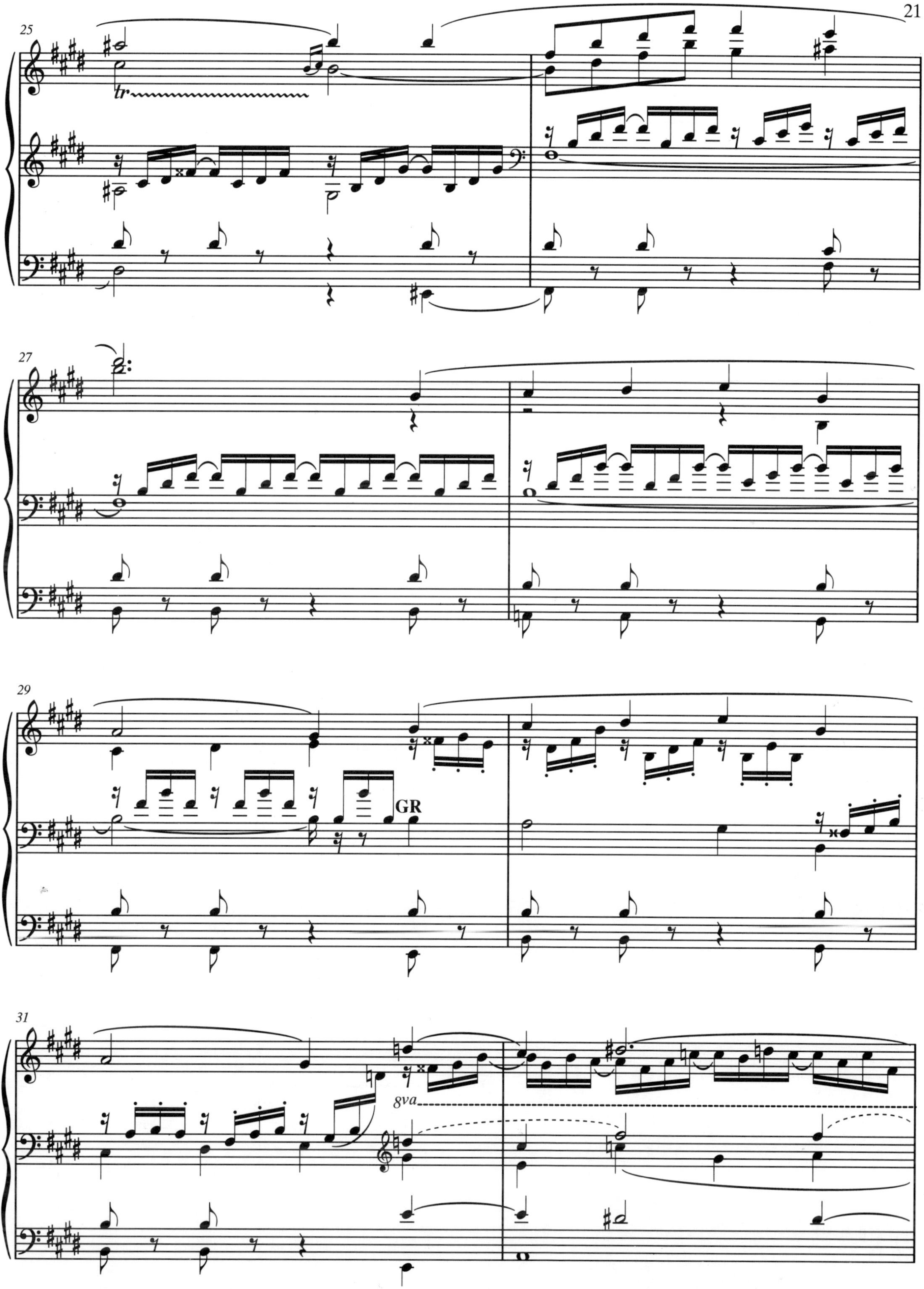
25
tr
27
29
GR
31
8va

33
(8va)
35
R
37
ritard.
39
Poco animato
P pp
GP
(G Bourdon 16', Flûte 8')
Péd. GP

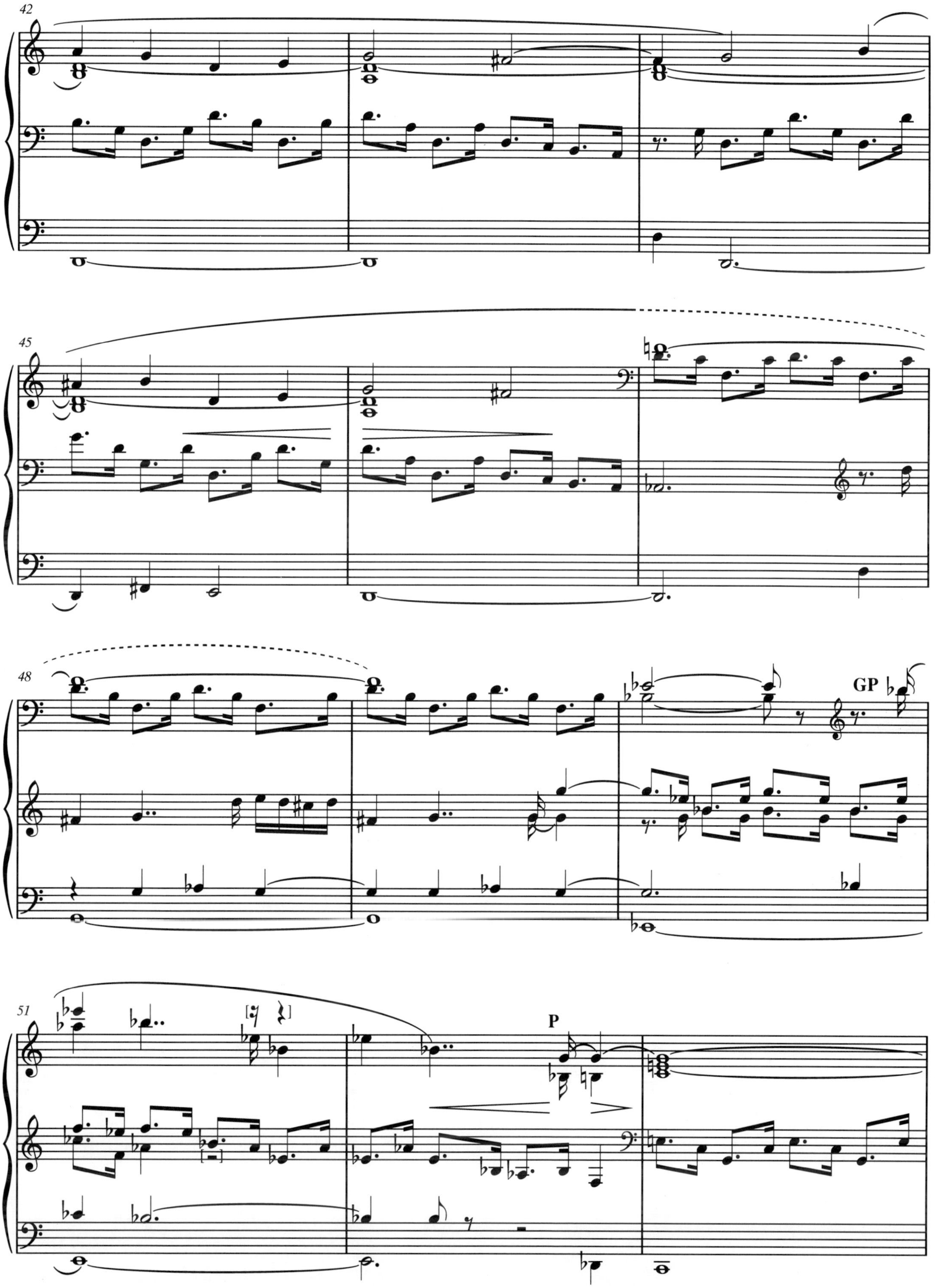
42
45
48
GP
51
P

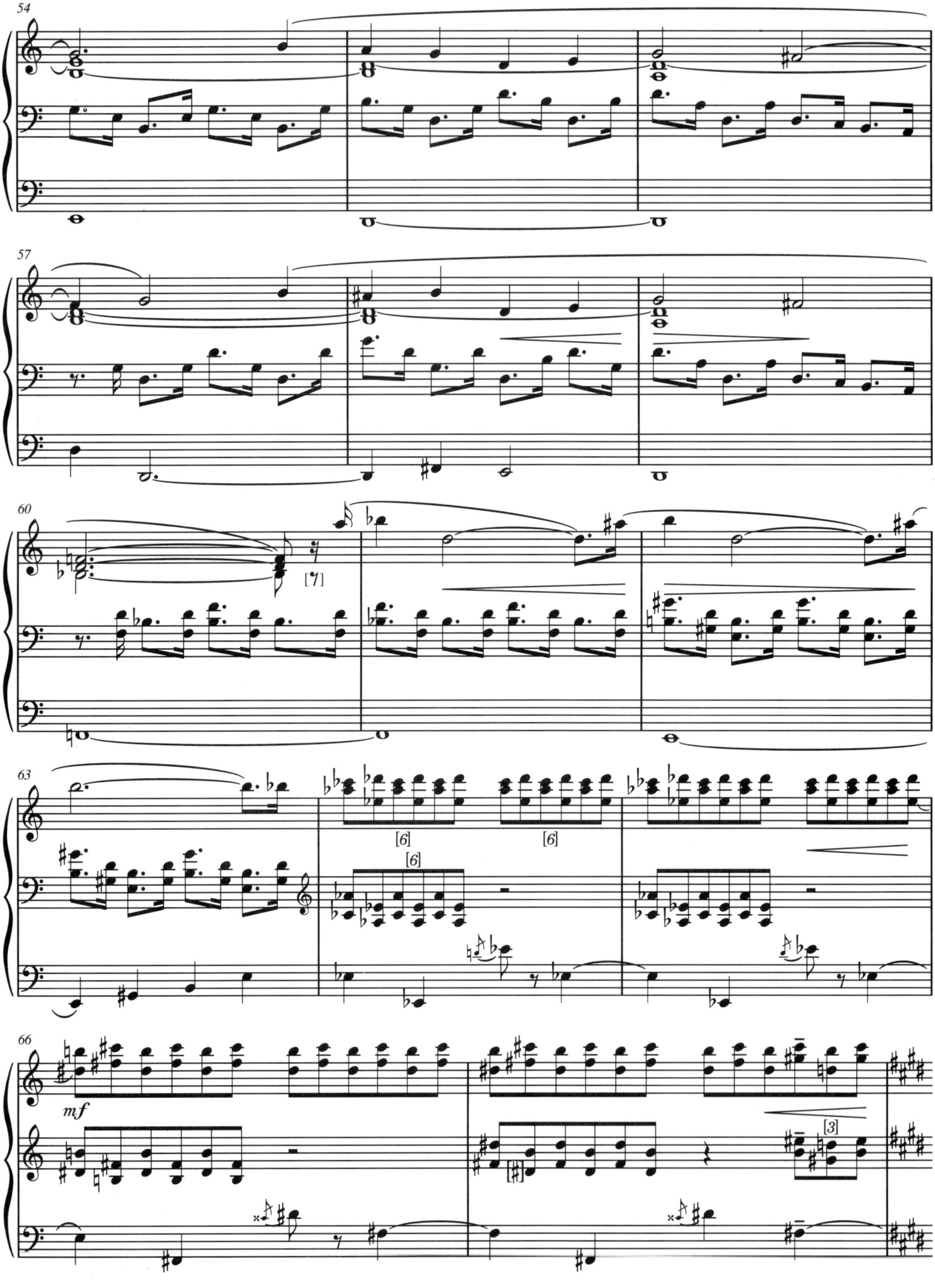
54
57
60
[7]
63
[6]
[6]
[6]
66
mf
[♯]
[3]

* See Critical Notes.

26

27

III

Grand orgue: Montre 8', Flûte 8',
       Prestant 4' (Anches 8', 4' préparés)
Positif: Salicional 8', Flûte 8' (Anches 8', 4' préparés)
Récit: Bourdon 8', Flûte 4', Octavin 2',
    Hautbois [8'] (Anches 8', 4' préparés)
Pédale: Basses 8'

Allegro (♩ = 132)

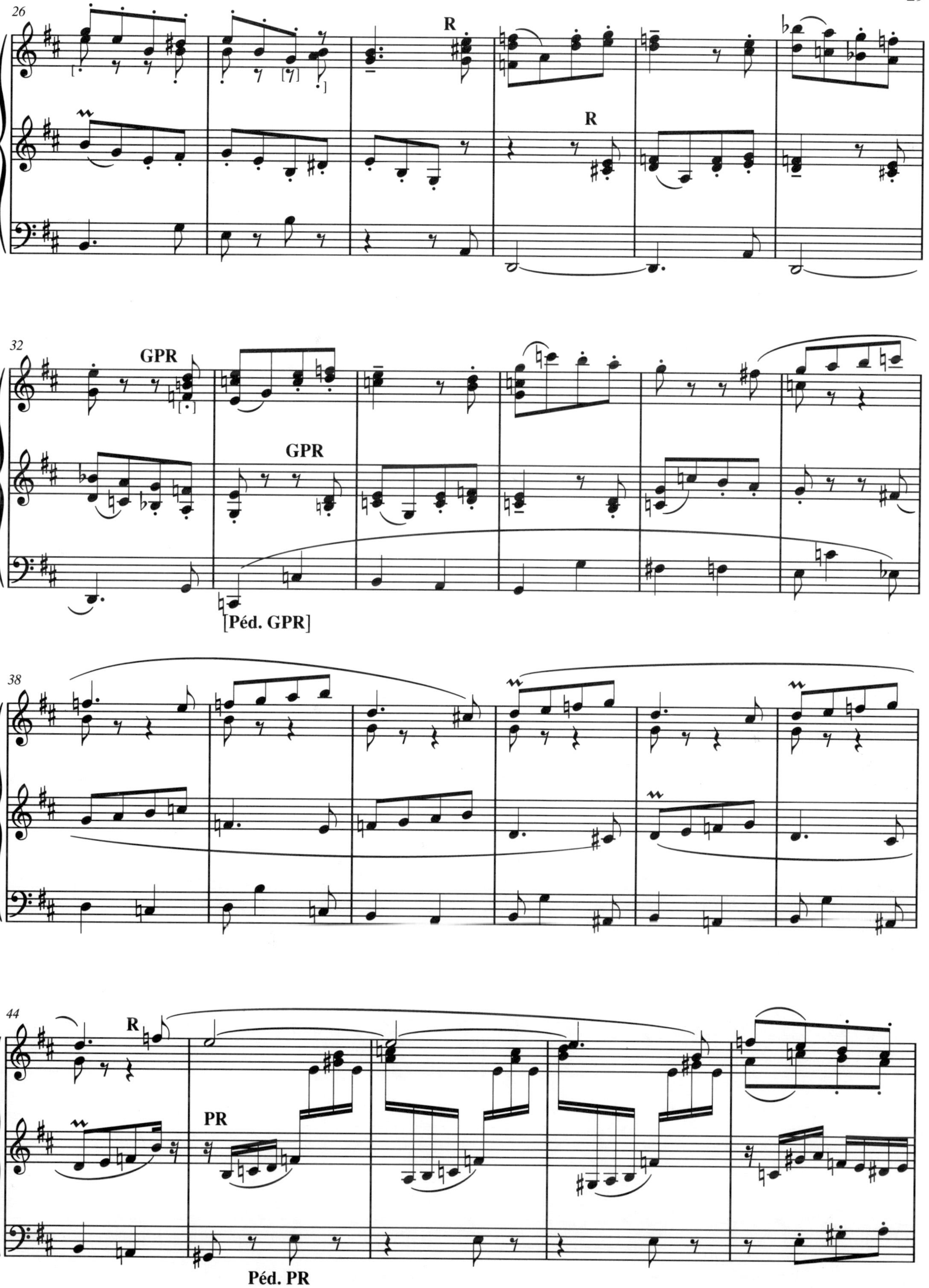
26
R
R
32
GPR
GPR
[Péd. GPR]
38
44
R
PR
Péd. PR

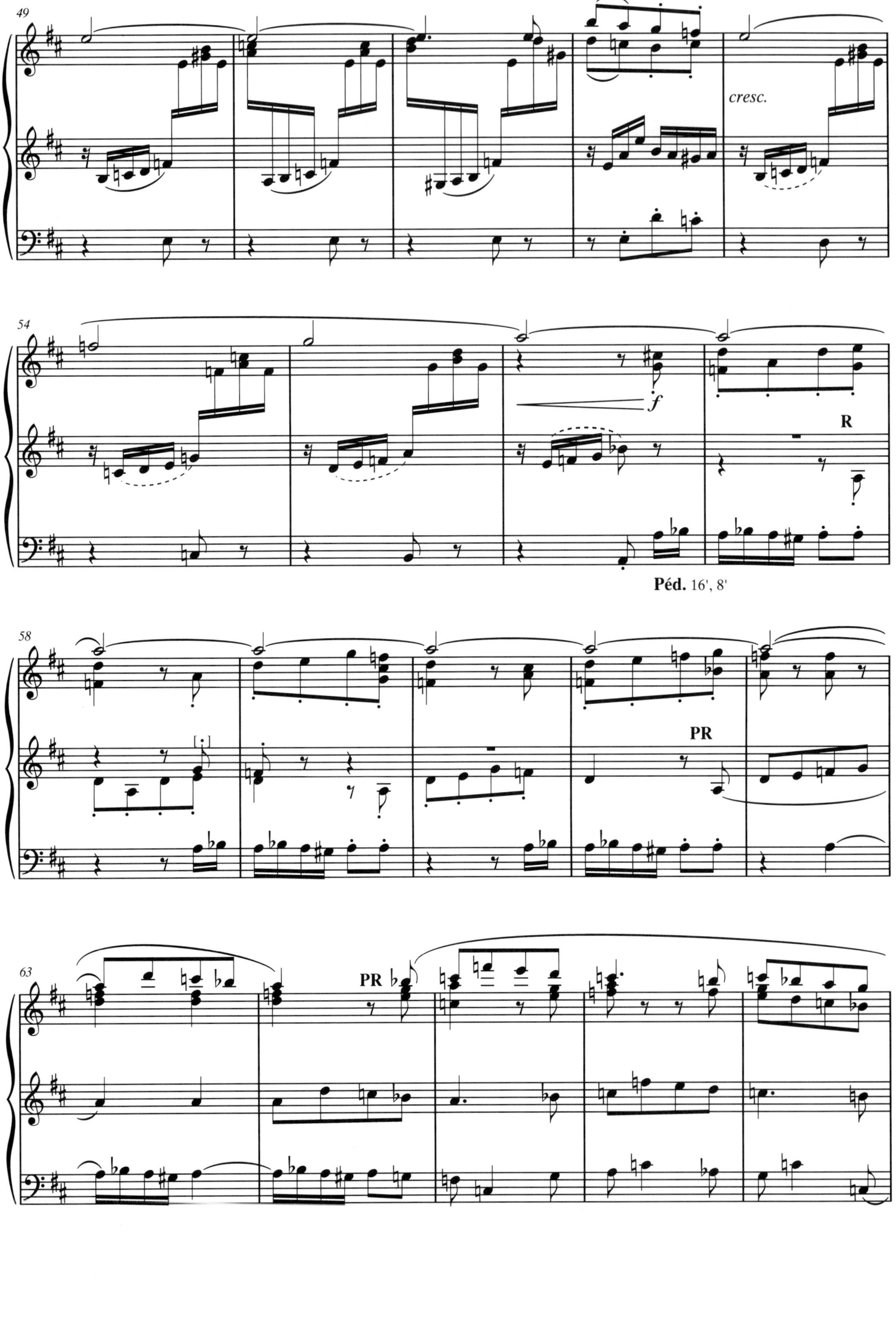
49
cresc.
54
f
R
Péd. 16', 8'
58
PR
63
PR

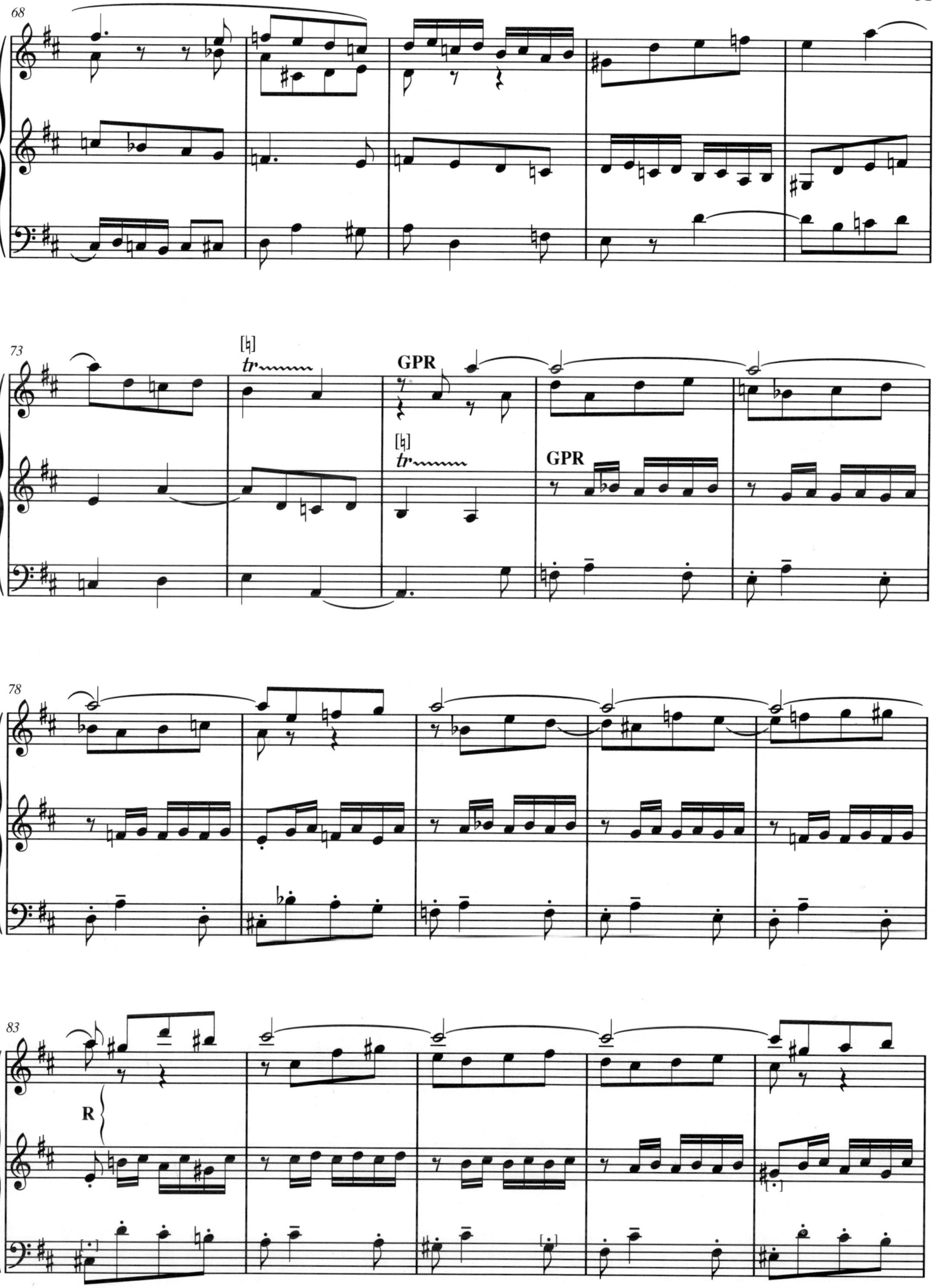
68
73
[♮]
tr
GPR
[♮]
tr
GPR
78
83
R

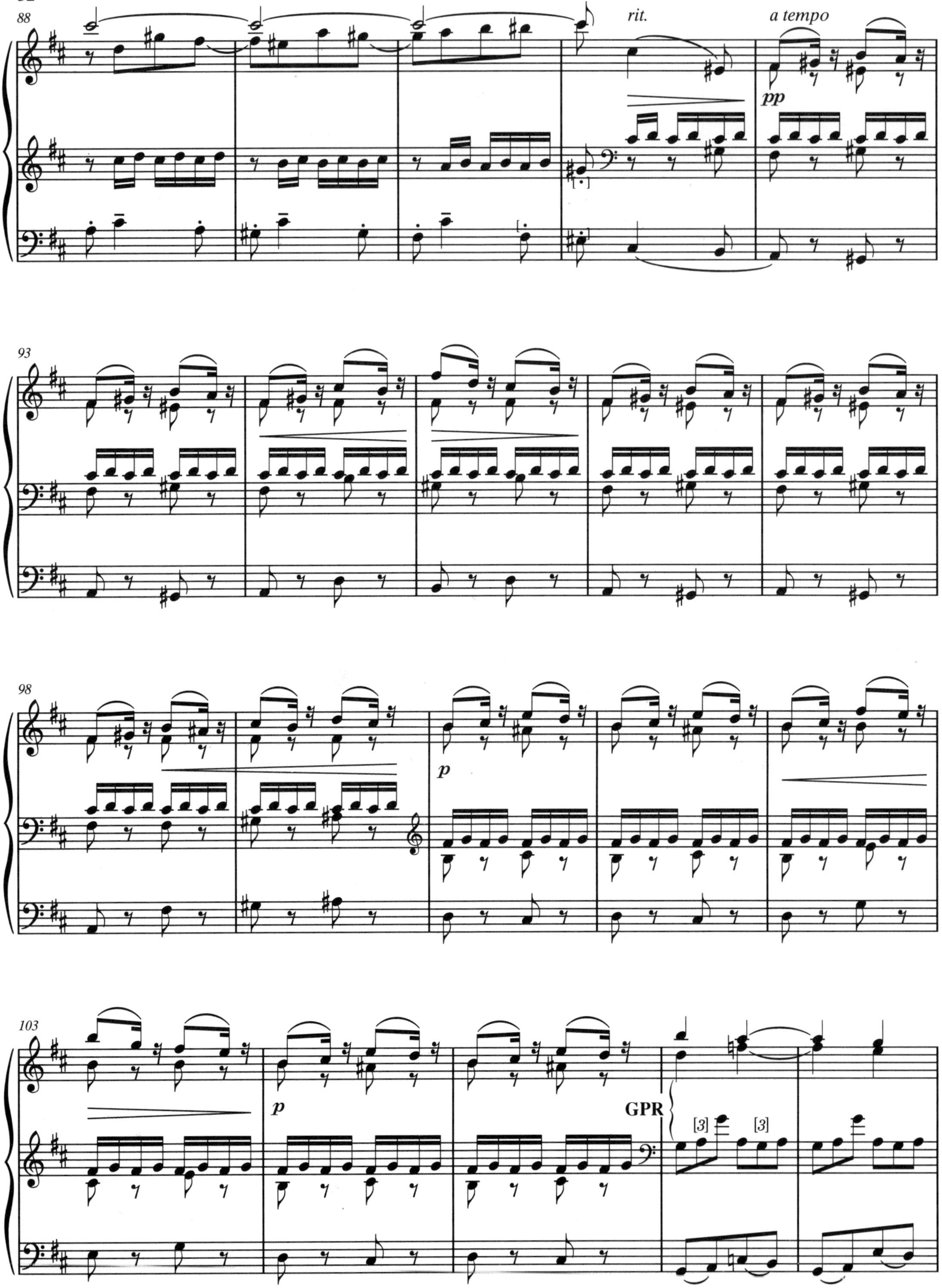
88
rit.
a tempo
pp
93
98
p
103
p
GPR
[3]
[3]

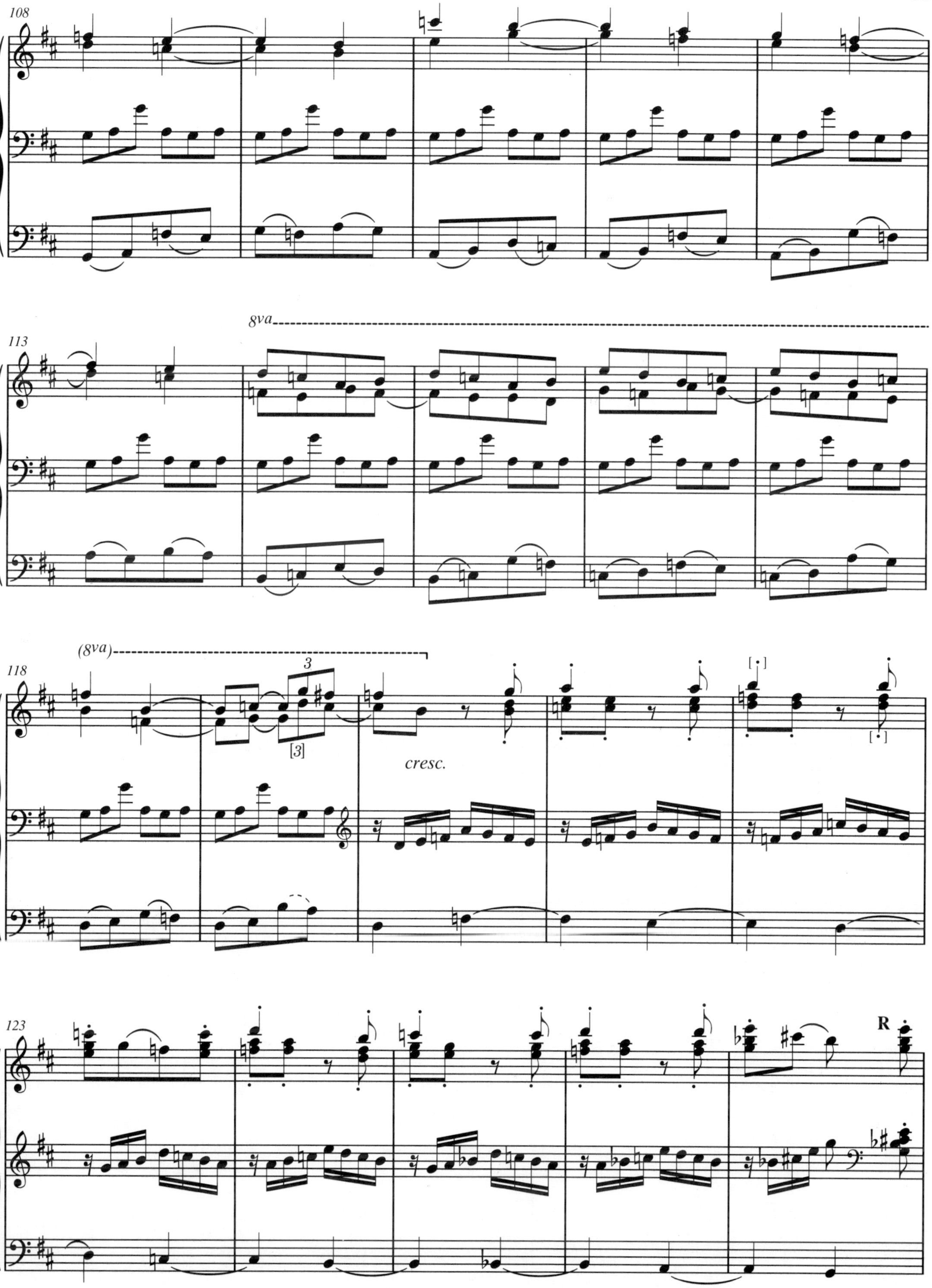
108
113
8va
(8va)
118
3
[3]
cresc.
[·]
123
R

34

[Anches Positif]*

*See Critical Notes for mm. 142–90.

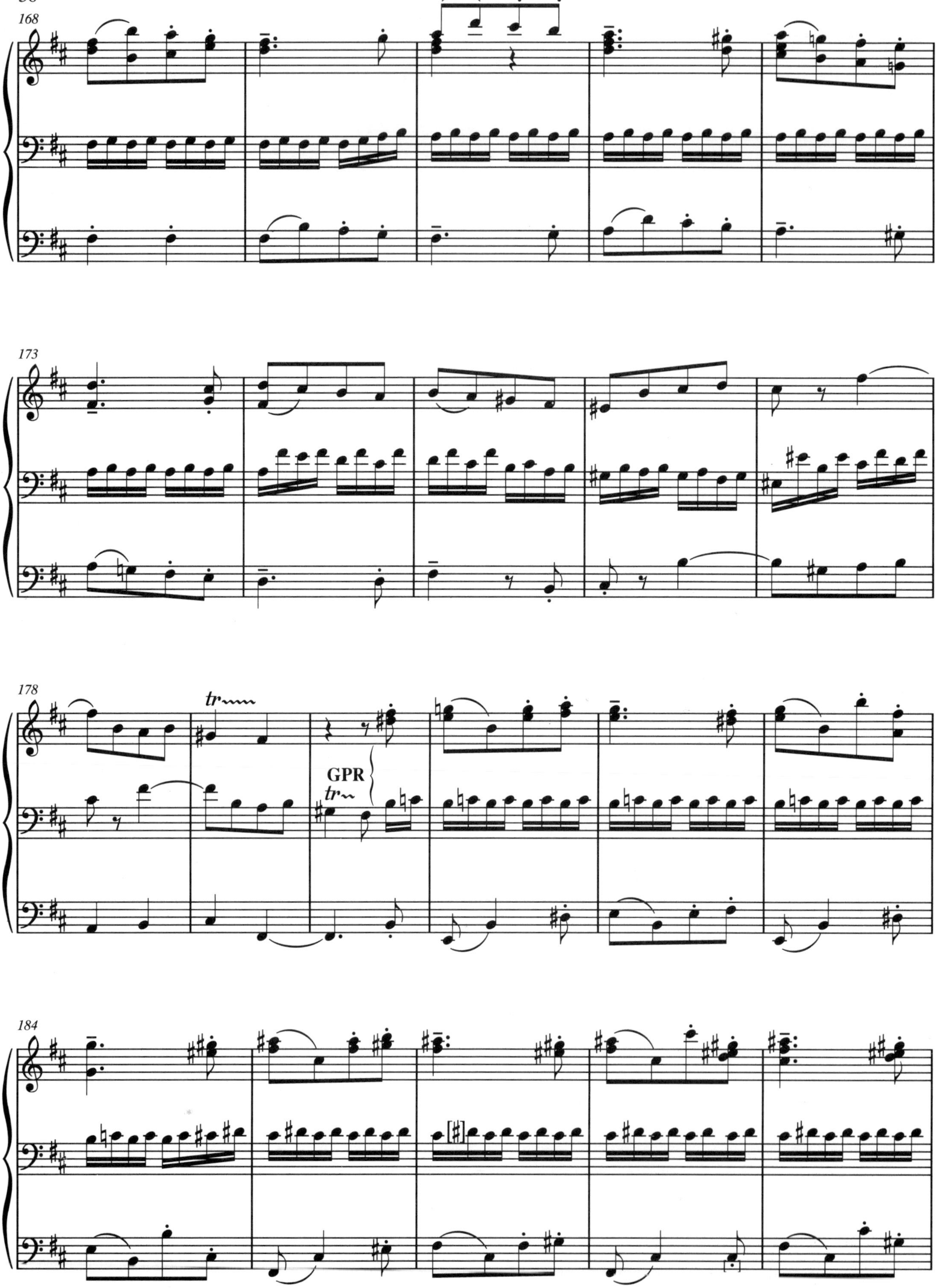
168
173
178
tr
GPR
tr
184

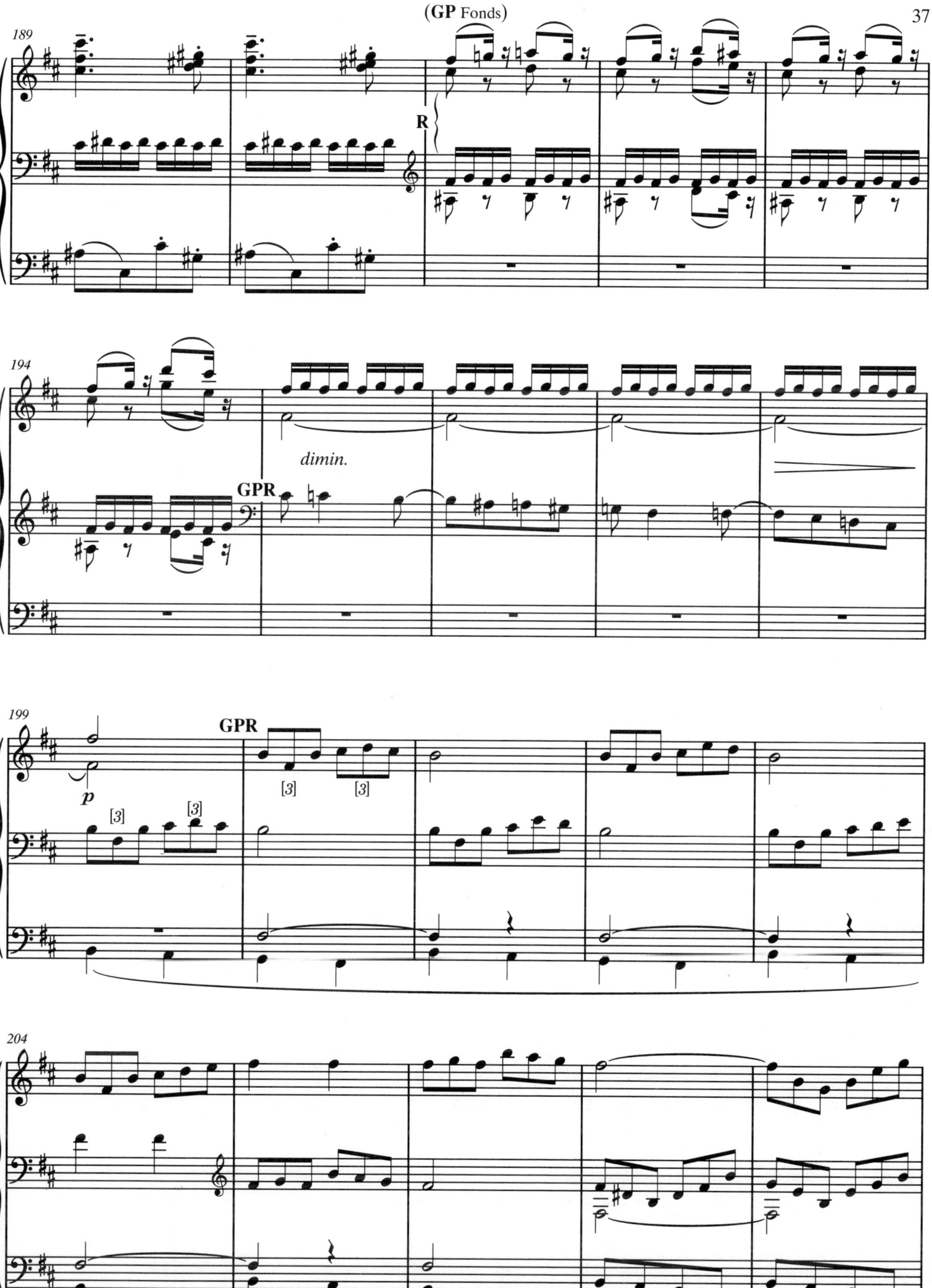
(GP Fonds)
189
R
194
GPR
dimin.
199
p
[3]
[3]
GPR
[3]
[3]
204

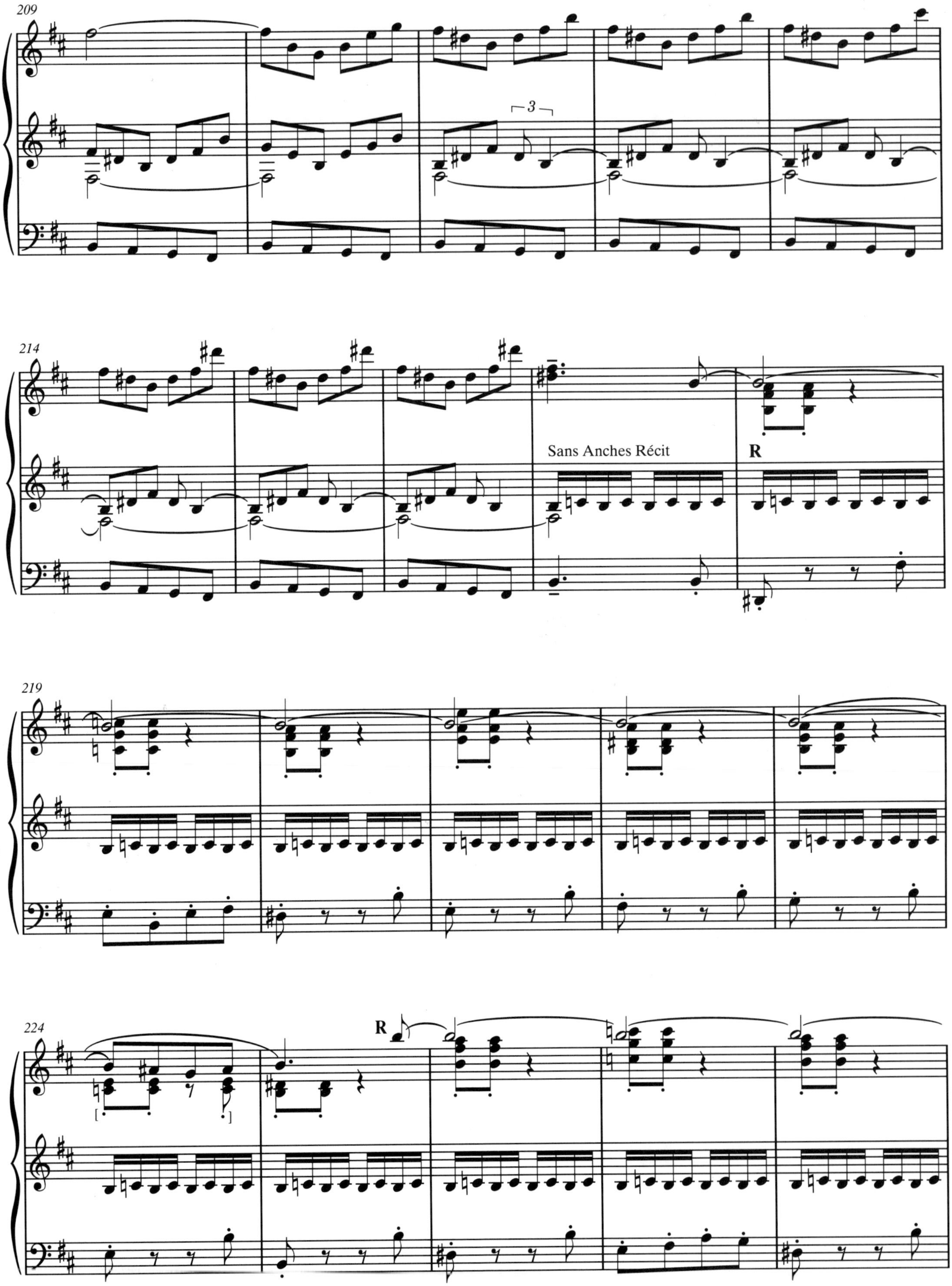
209
3
214
Sans Anches Récit
R
219
224
R

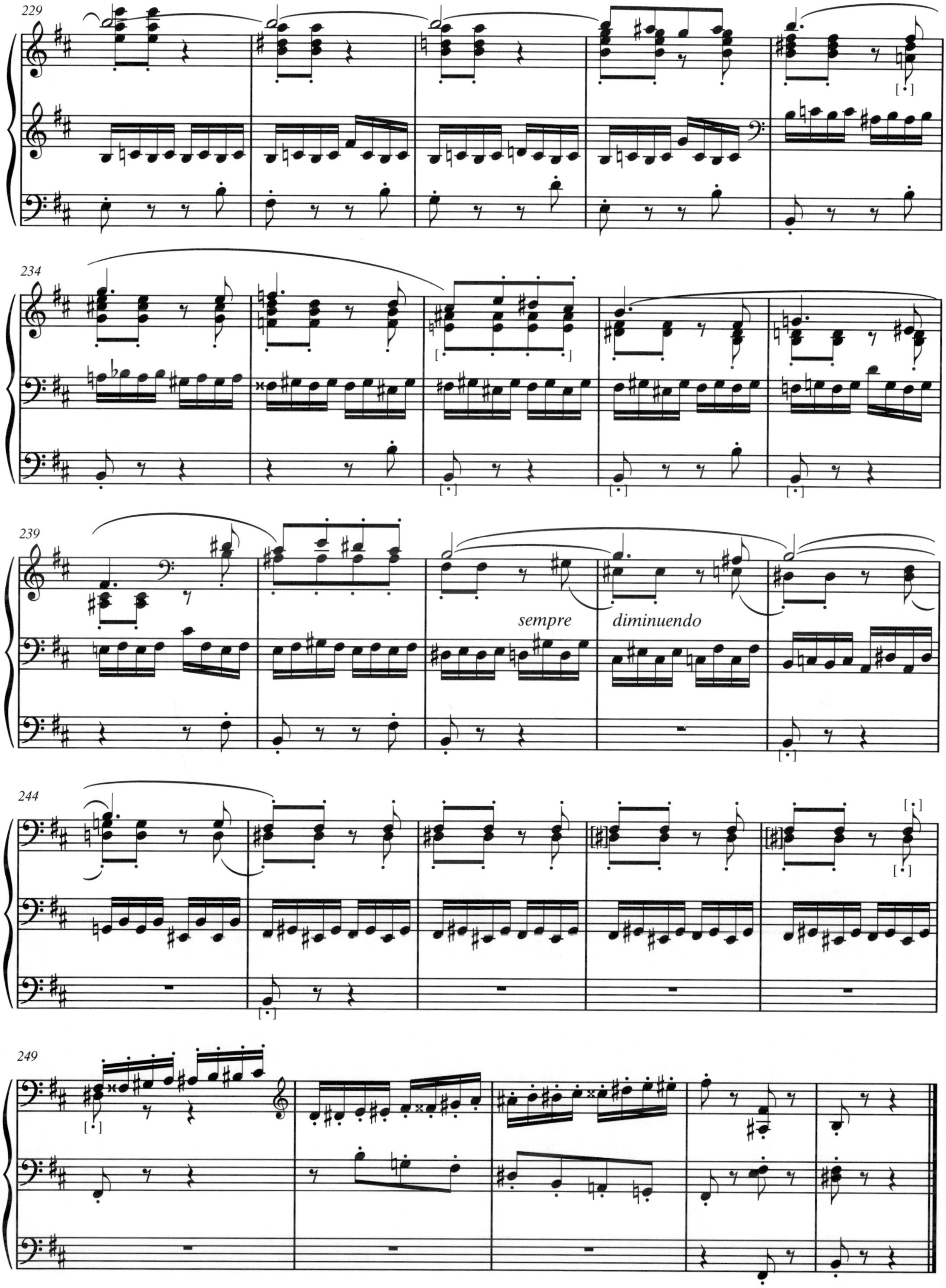
229
234
239
sempre
diminuendo
244
249

Grand orgue: Fonds 16', 8', 4'
Positif: Fonds 8', 4'
Récit: Fonds et Anches 16', 8', 4'
Pédale: Fonds 32', 16', 8', 4'

IV. Variations

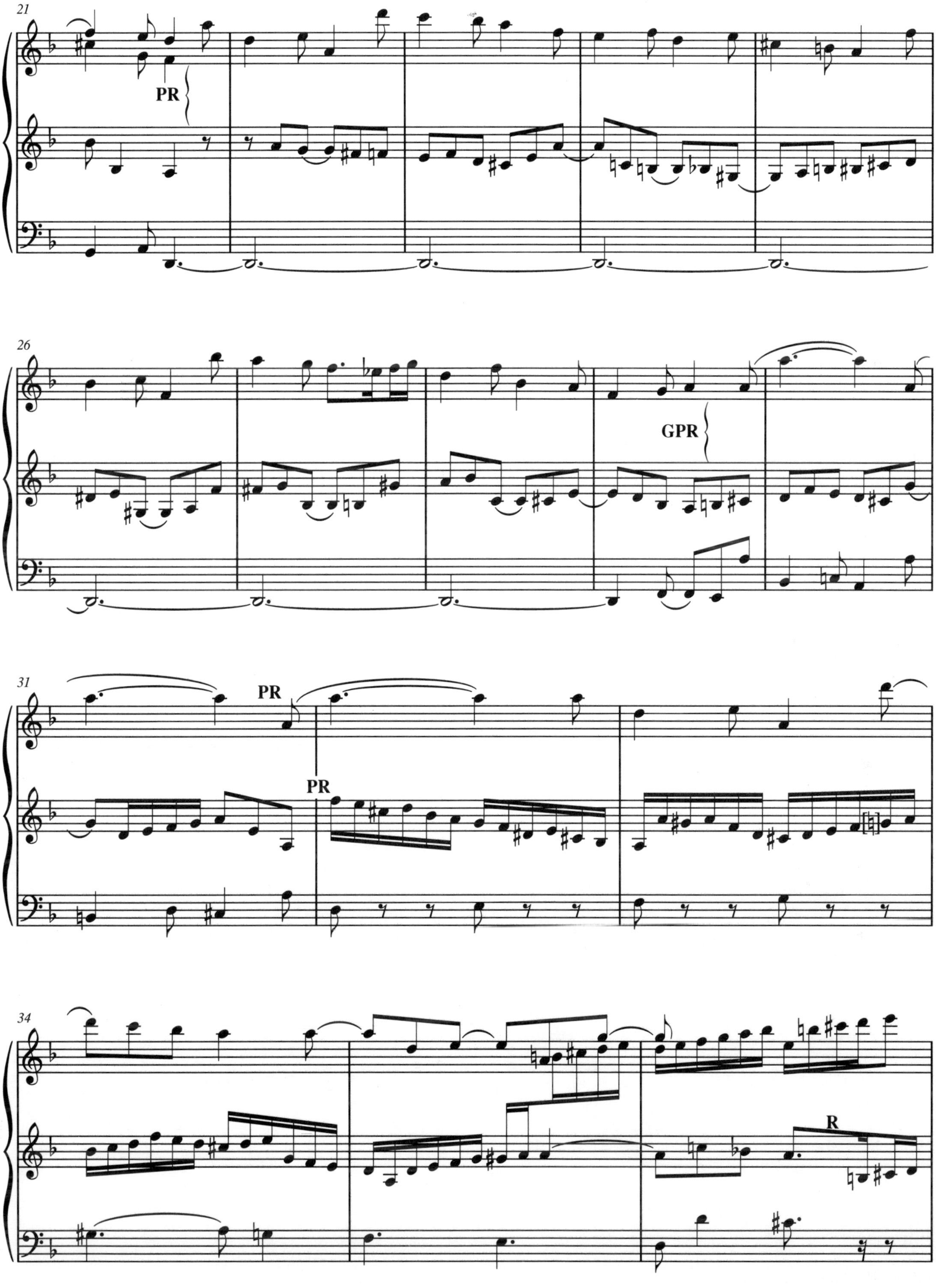
21
PR
26
GPR
31
PR
PR
34
R

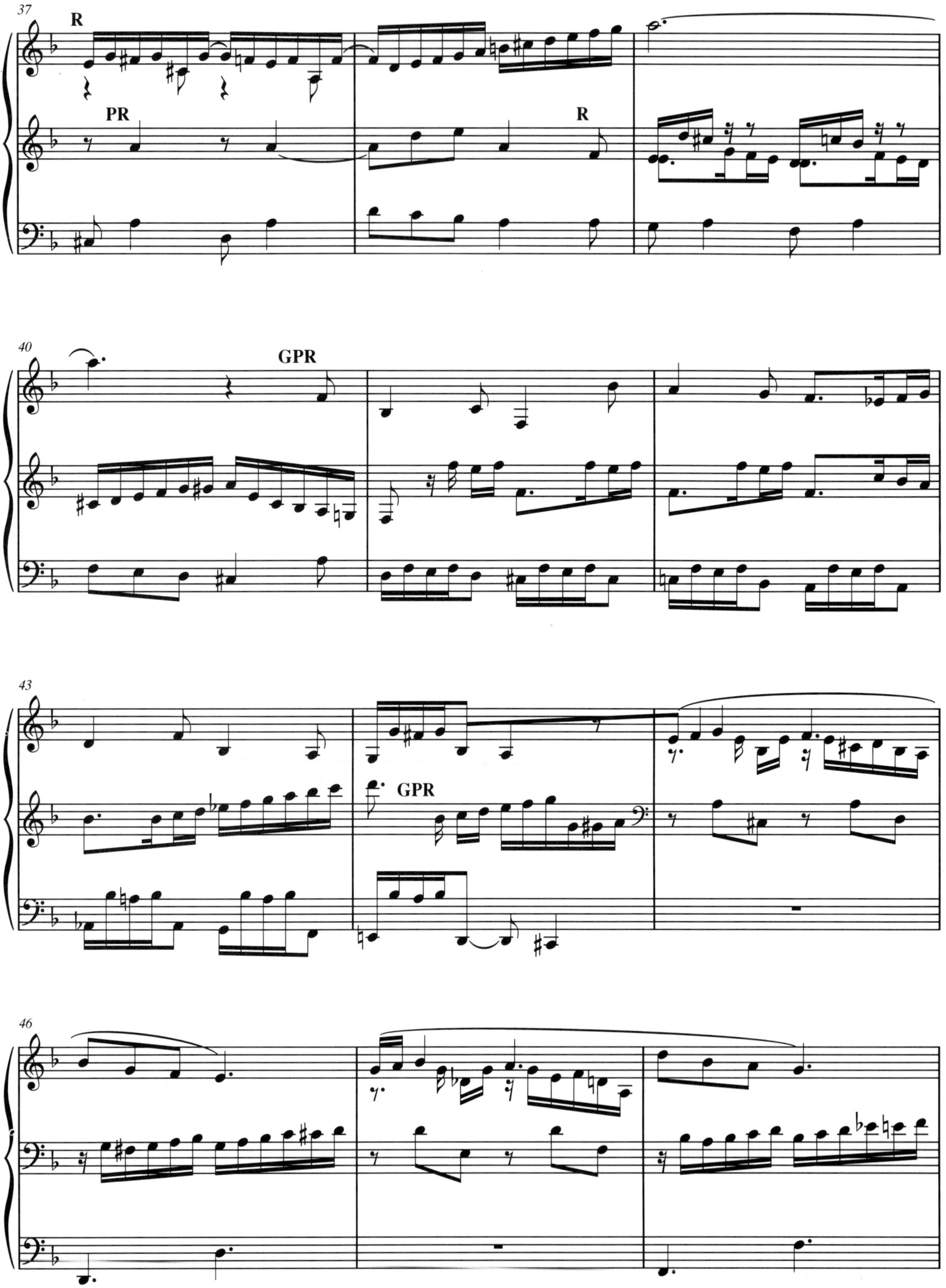
37
R
PR
R
40
GPR
43
GPR
46

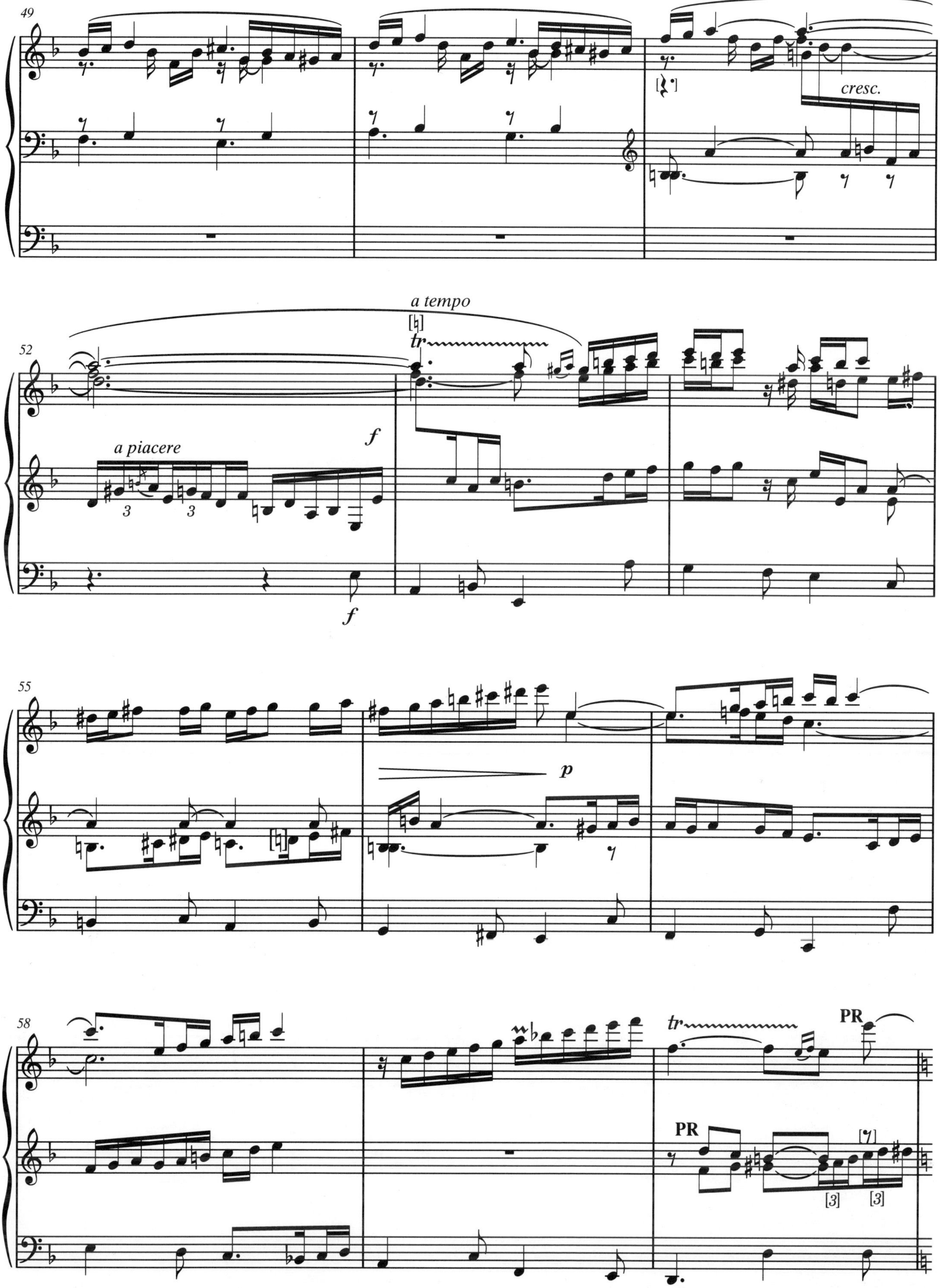
49
cresc.
52
a tempo
a piacere
f
55
p
58
PR

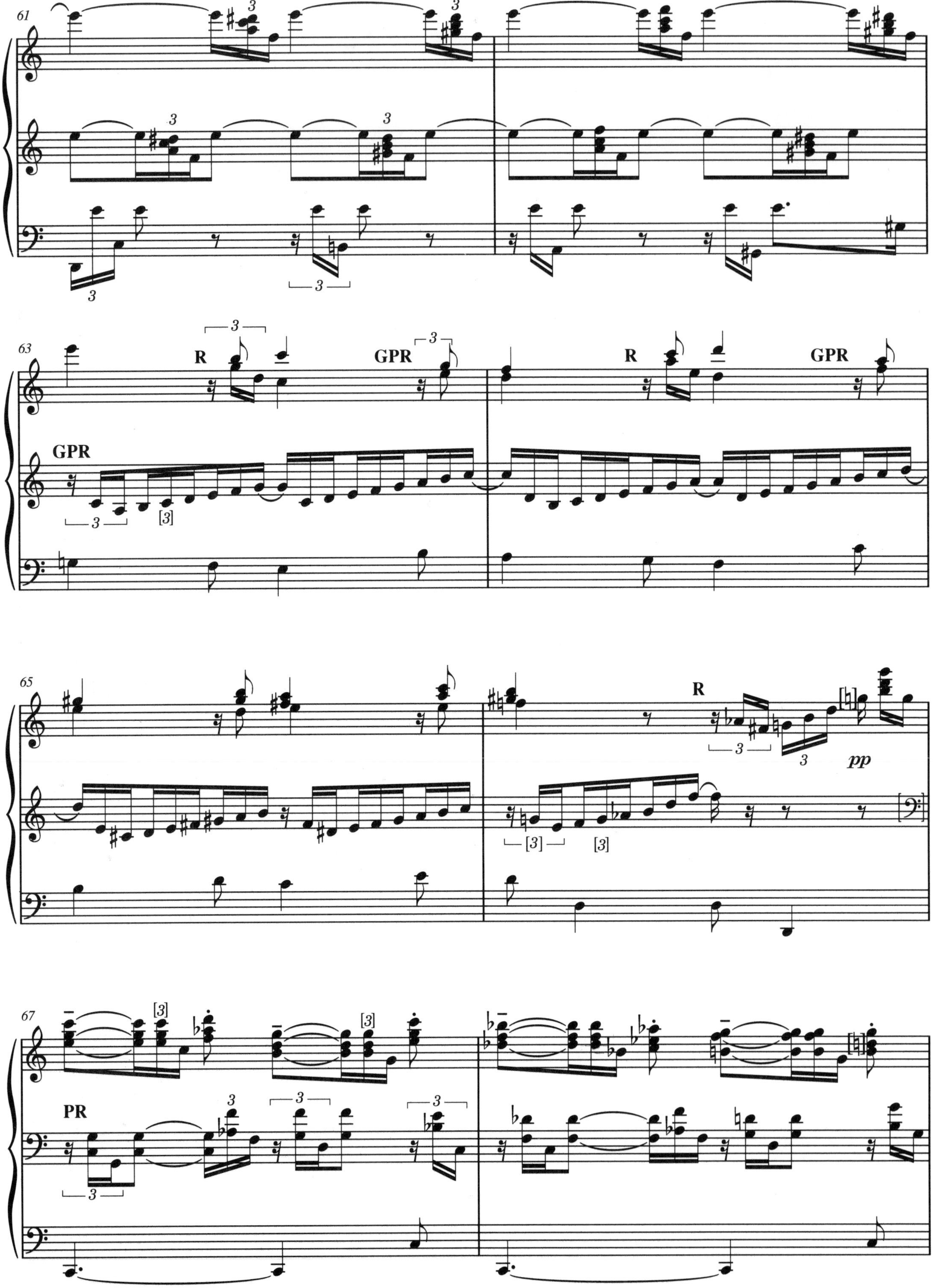

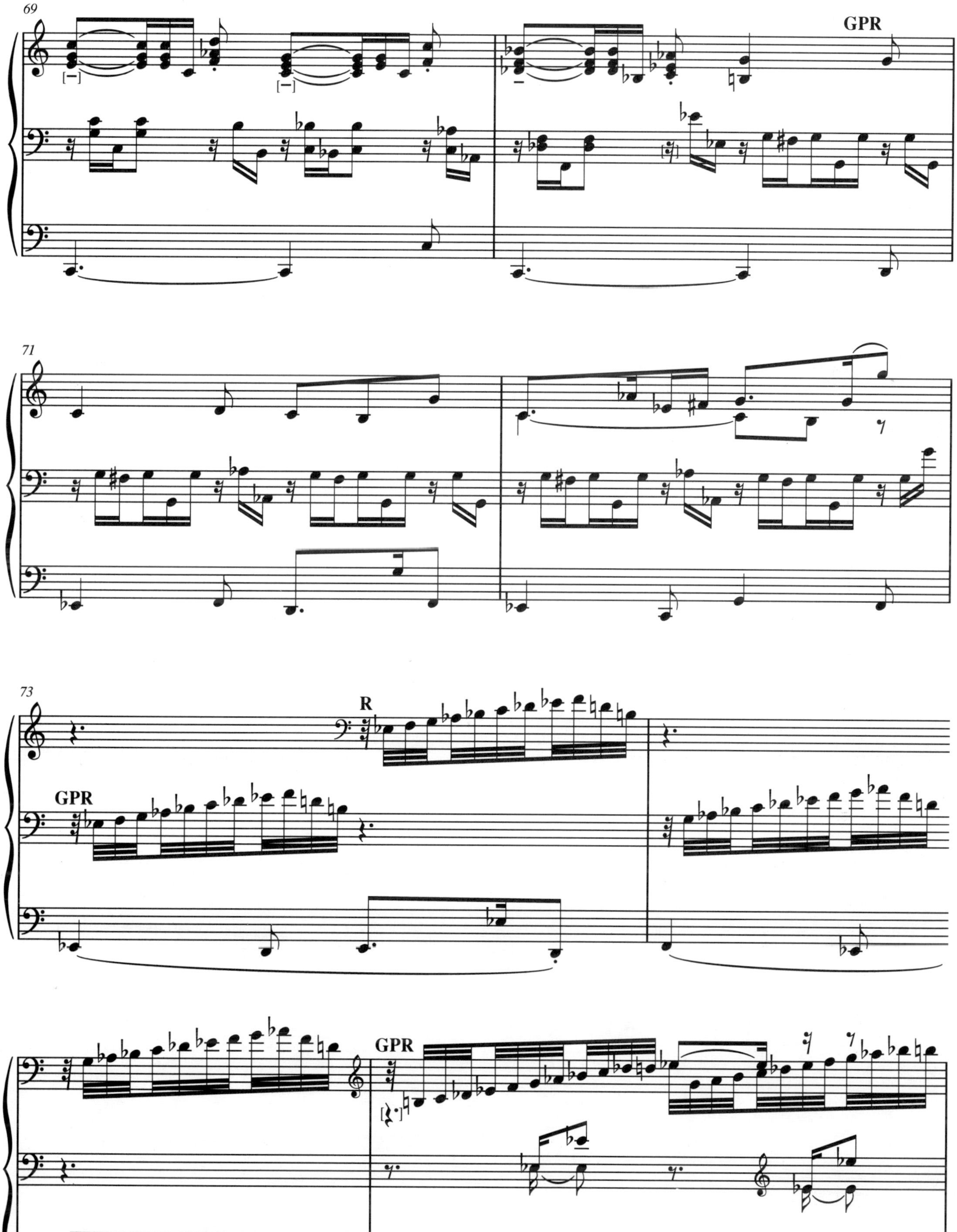
69
GPR
71
73
R
GPR
GPR

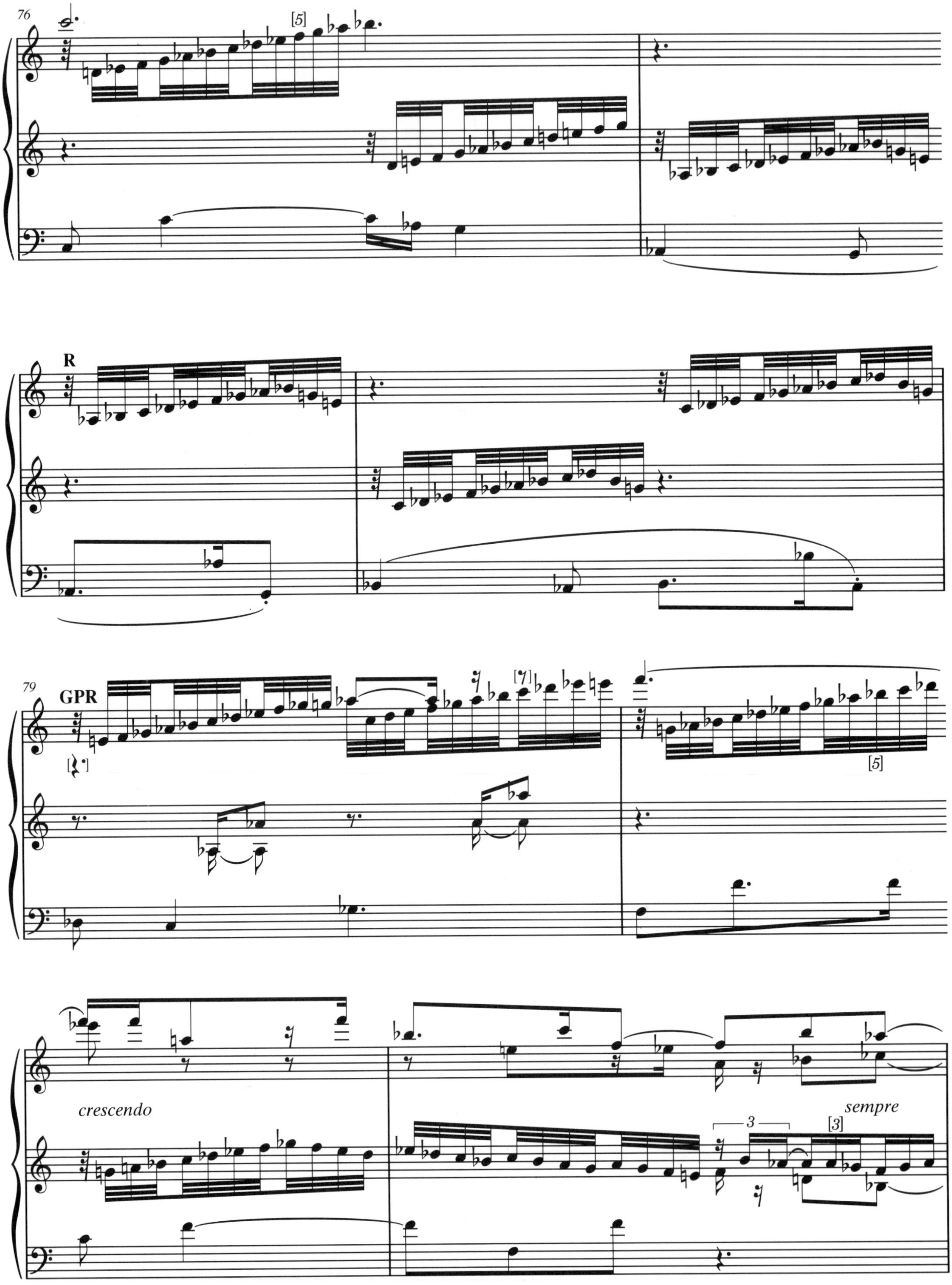

76
[5]
R
79
GPR
[7]
[5]
crescendo
3
sempre
[3]

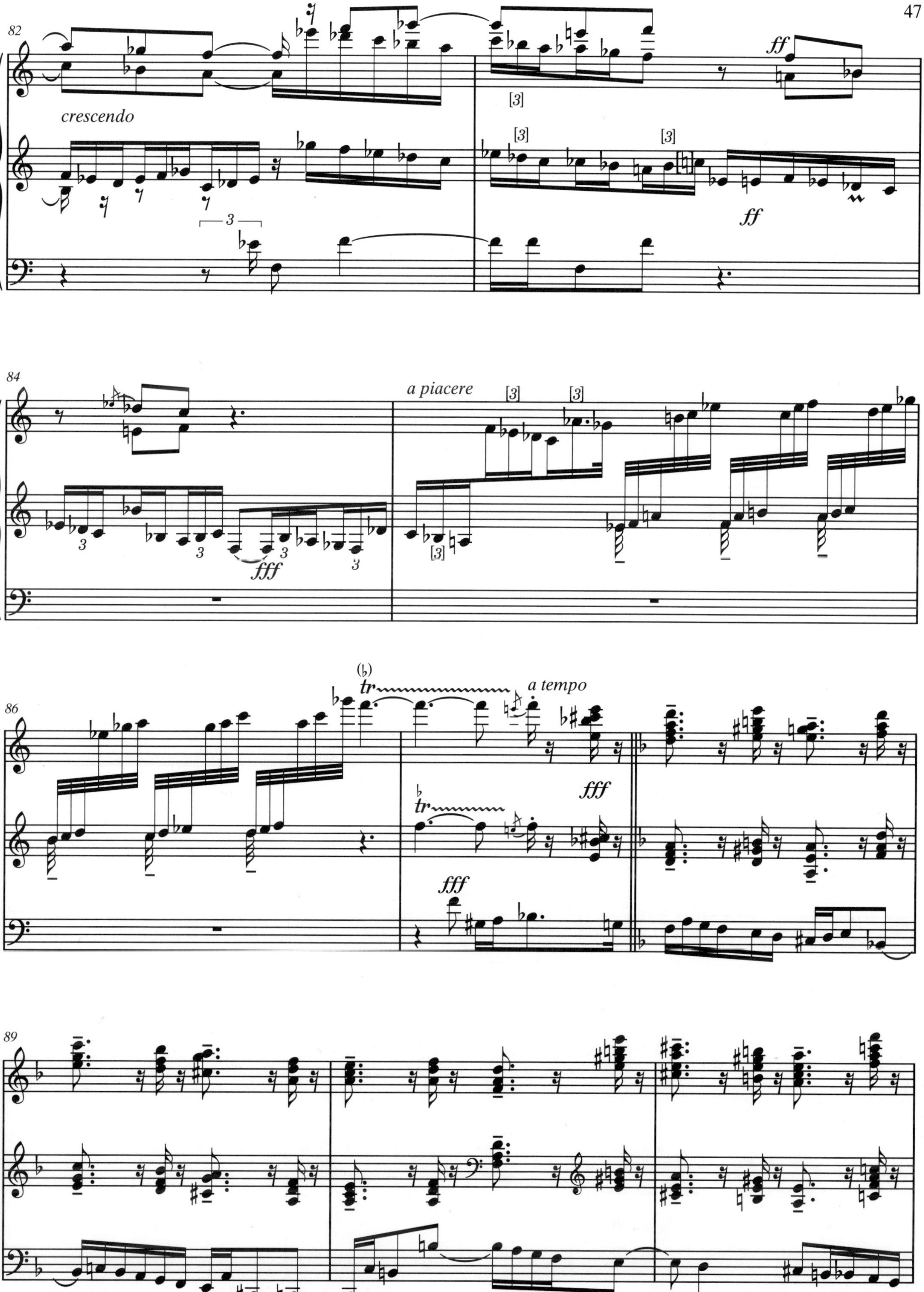
82
crescendo
[3]
ff
84
a piacere
fff
86
tr
a tempo
fff
89

Supprimez peu à peu

les Anches de la **Pédale,** du **Grand-orgue** et du **Positif** *

* Little by little supress the reeds of the Pédale, Grand-orgue, and Positif

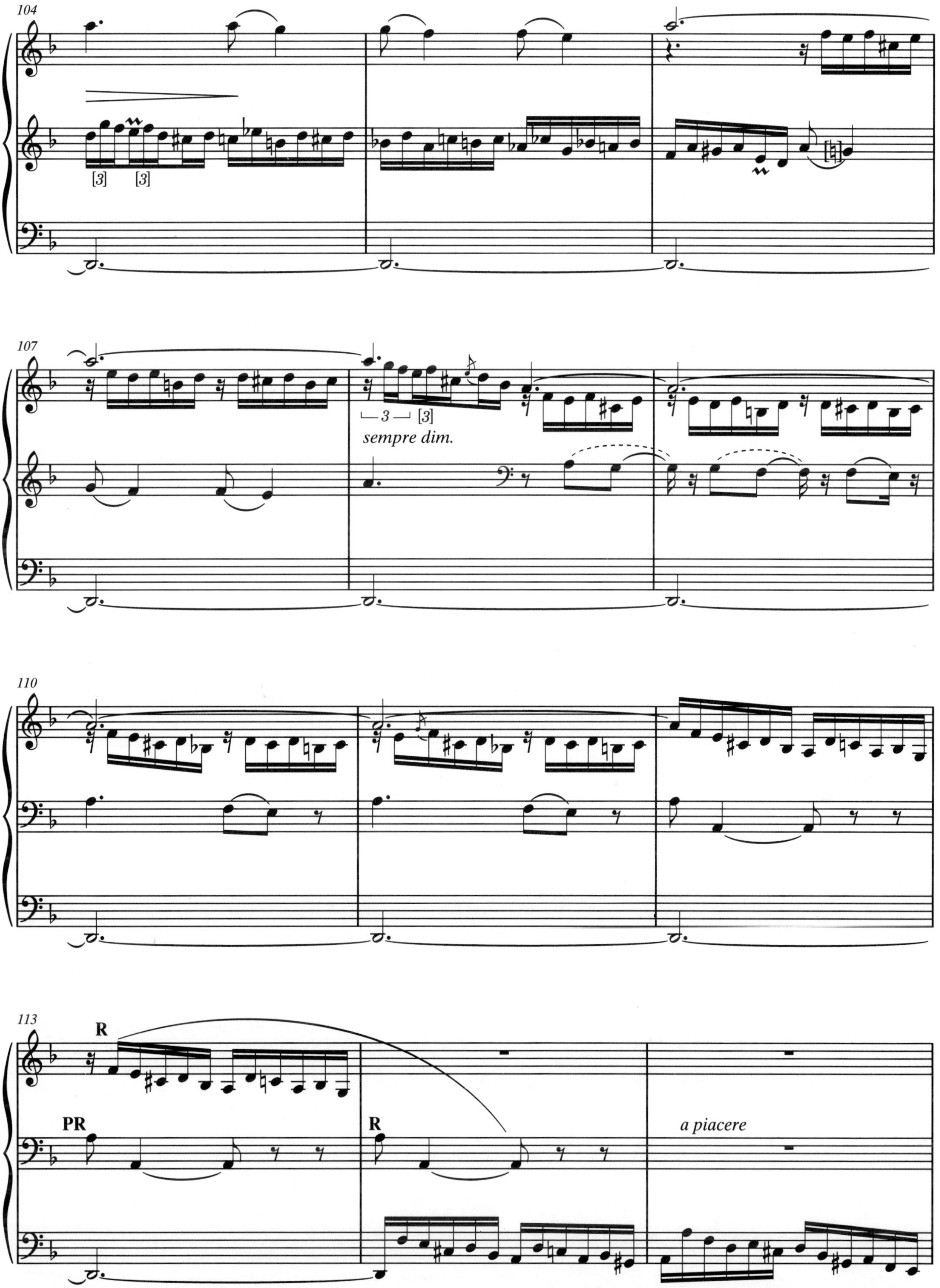
104
[3]
[3]
107
3
[3]
sempre dim.
110
113
R
PR
R
a piacere

a tempo ma un poco più animato (♩. = 48)
116
(R Hautbois)
R
p
(P Flûte 8')
P
(Péd. Flûte 8')
120
124
Péd. solo
127
[3]

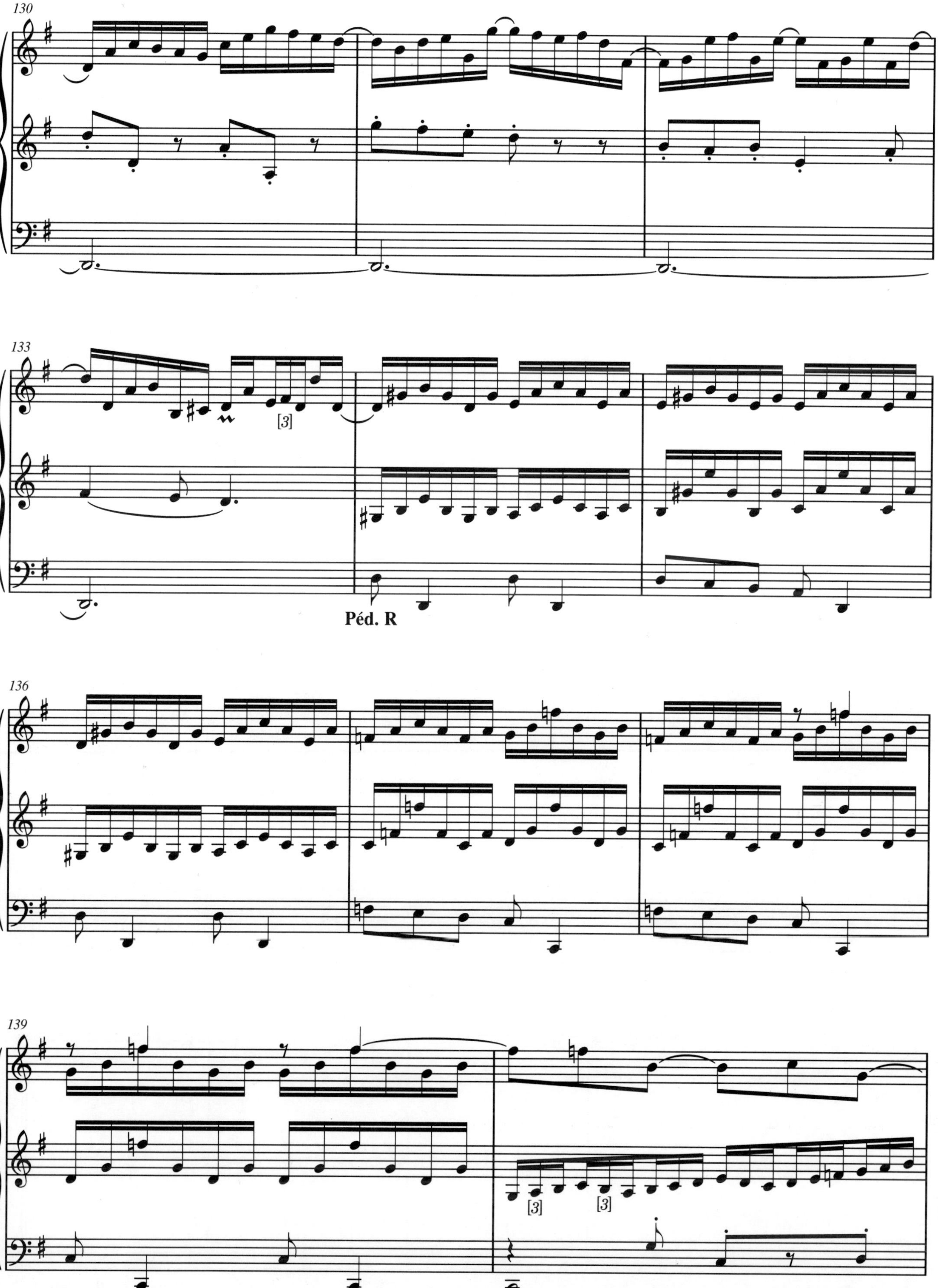
130
133
[3]
Péd. R
136
139
[3]
[3]

141
143
[3]
[3]
145
tr
rit.
148
a piacere
(GP Fonds 8')
rit.
(R Anches 16', 8', 4')
G
a tempo
G
[𝄽.]
[𝄾]
(Péd. Fonds 16', 8', 4')
Péd. G

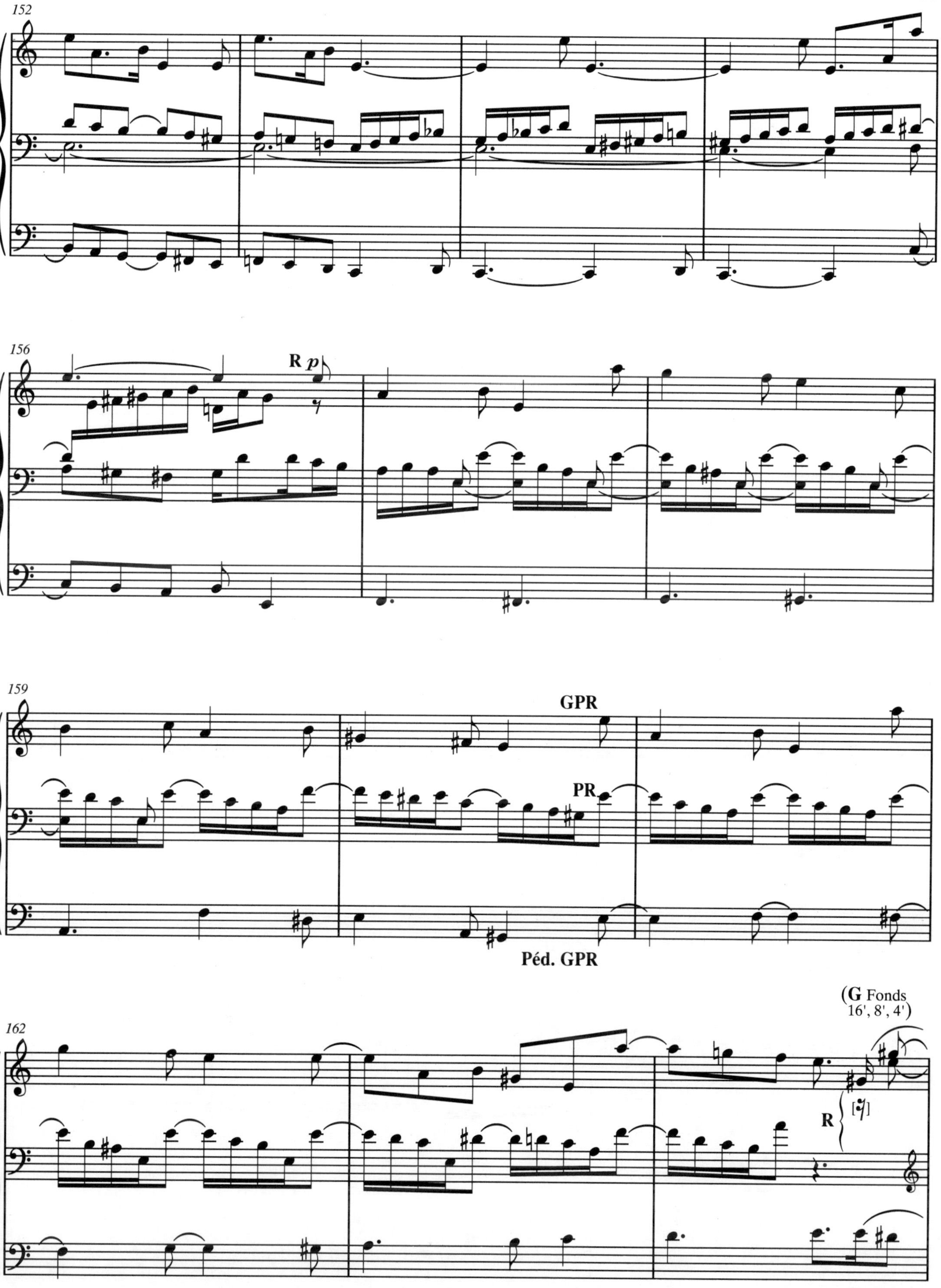
152
156
R p
159
GPR
PR
Péd. GPR
162
(G Fonds
16', 8', 4')
R

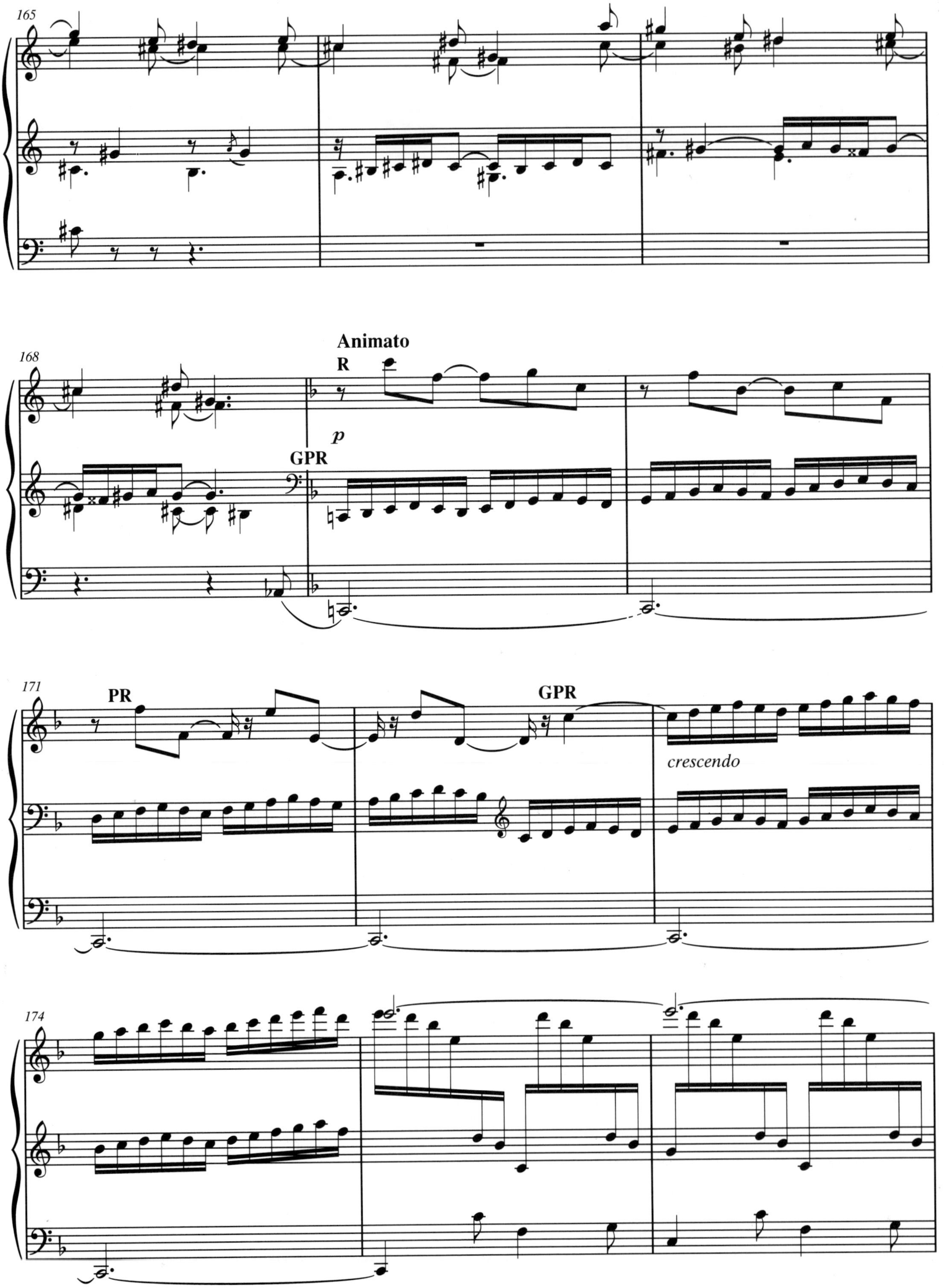
165
168
Animato
R
p
GPR
171
PR
GPR
crescendo
174

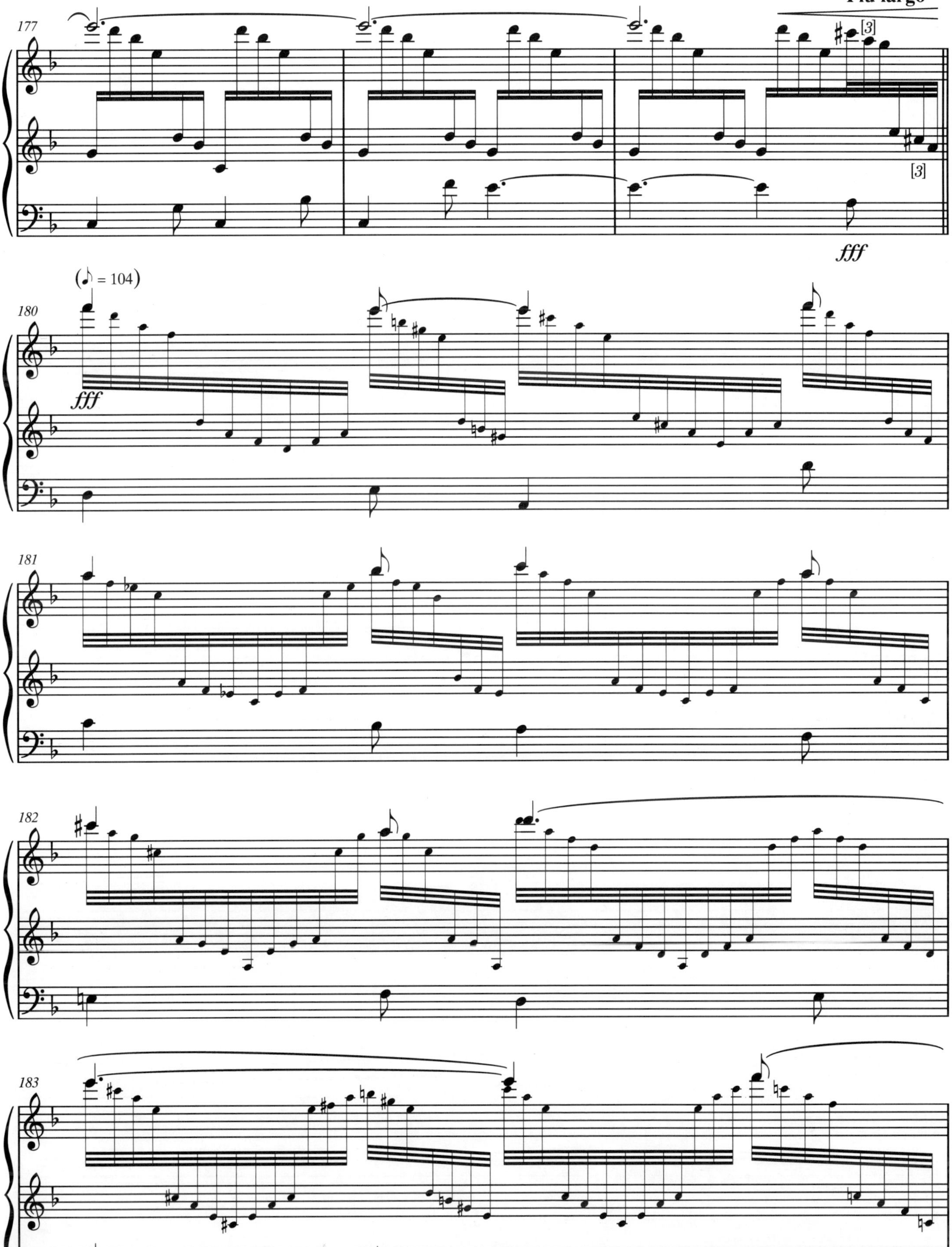

Più largo
177
[3]
[3]
fff
(♪ = 104)
180
fff
181
182
183

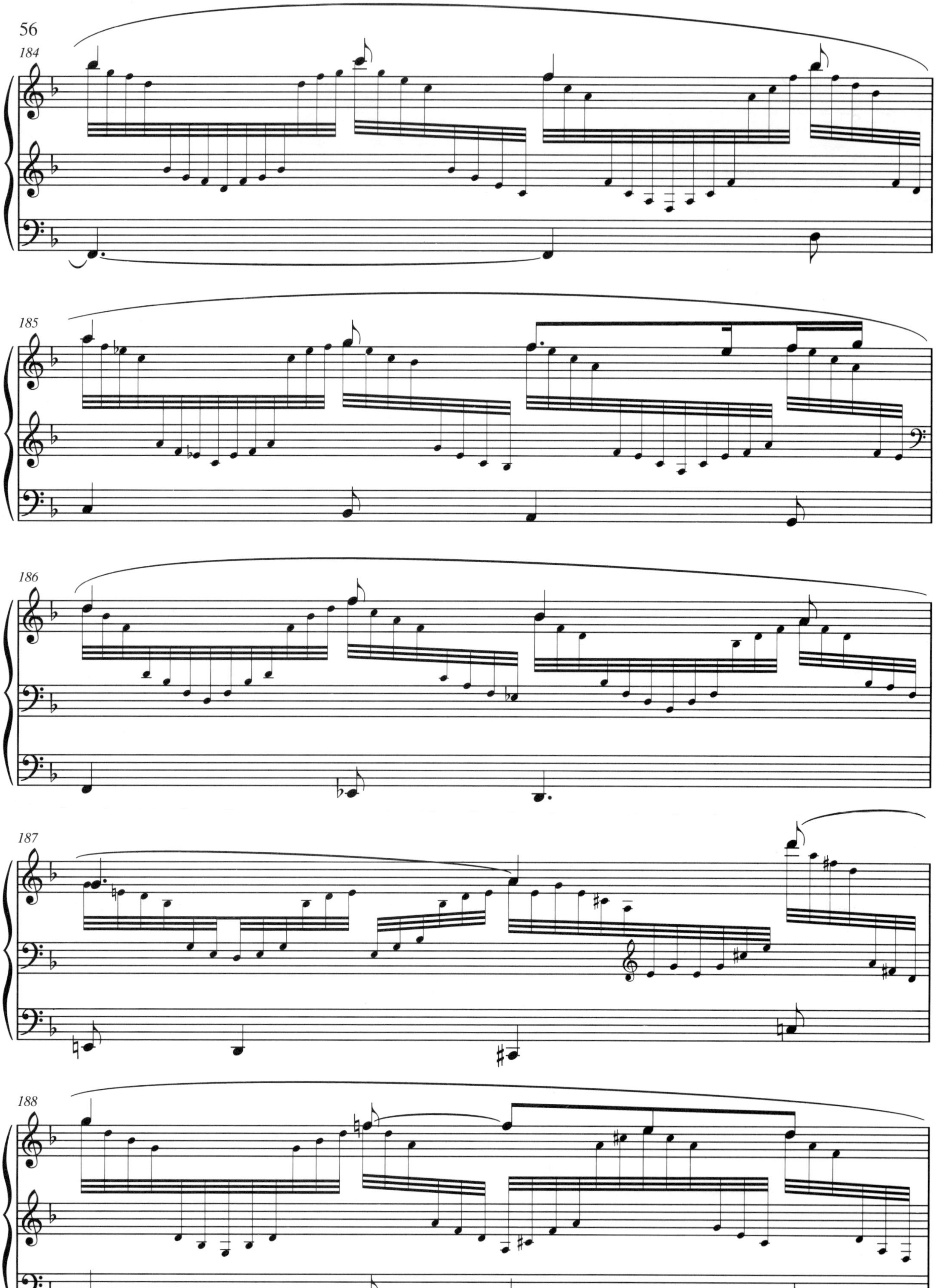
184
185
186
187
188

*Little by little suppress the reeds of the Pédale, Grand-orgue, and Positif

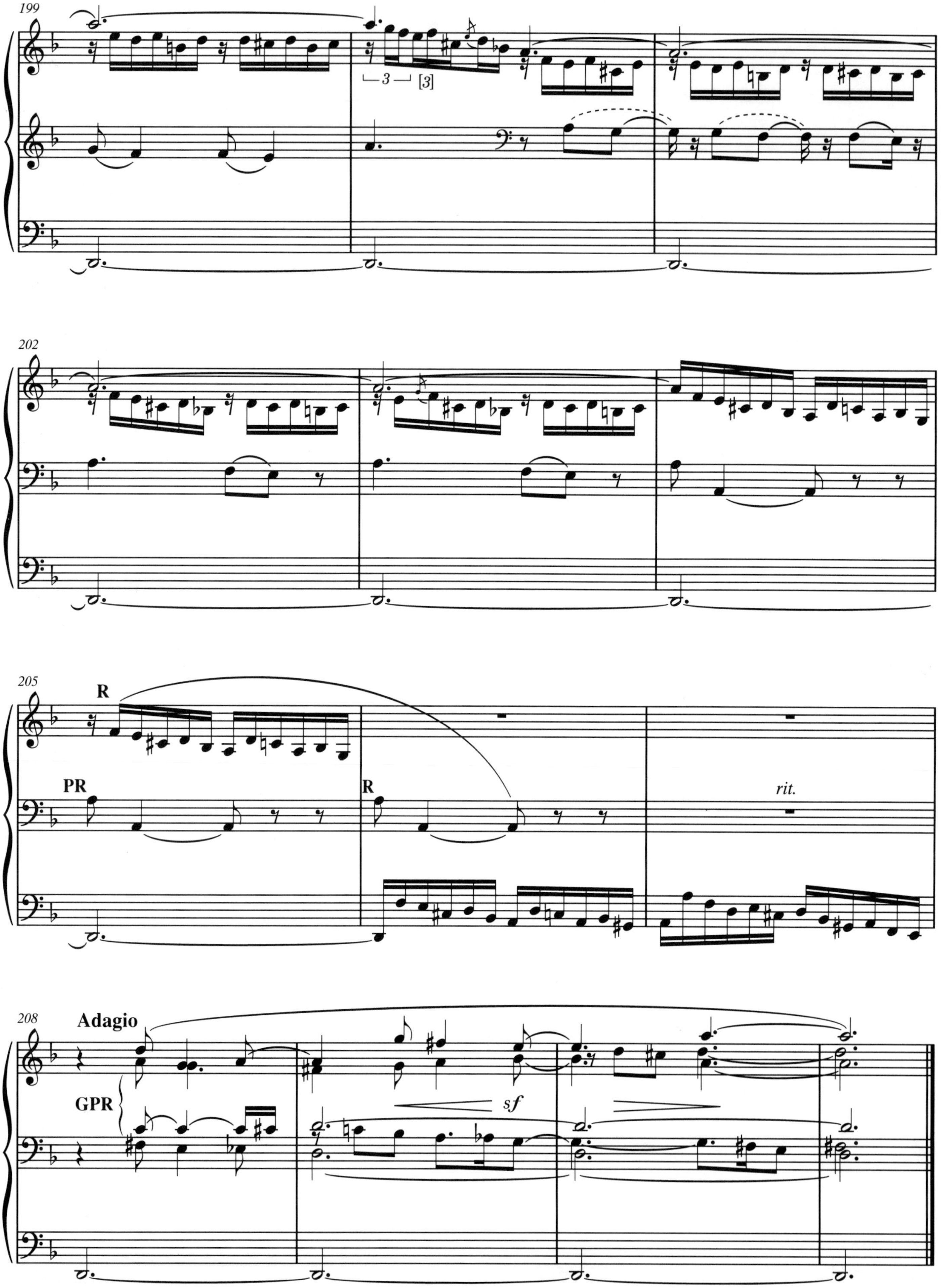
199
3
[3]
202
205
R
PR
R
rit.
208
Adagio
GPR
sf

Grand orgue: Fonds 8'
Positif: Fonds 8'
Récit: Flûtes, Gambes,
 Voix célestes 8' (Trompette préparée)
Pédale: Soubasse 16', Basses 8'

V. Adagio

61

27
30
ritard.
(G Fonds 16', 8', 4')
(R Hautbois, Flûtes 8', 4')
P
pp
R
pp
a tempo ma un poco agitato
Péd. P
34
37

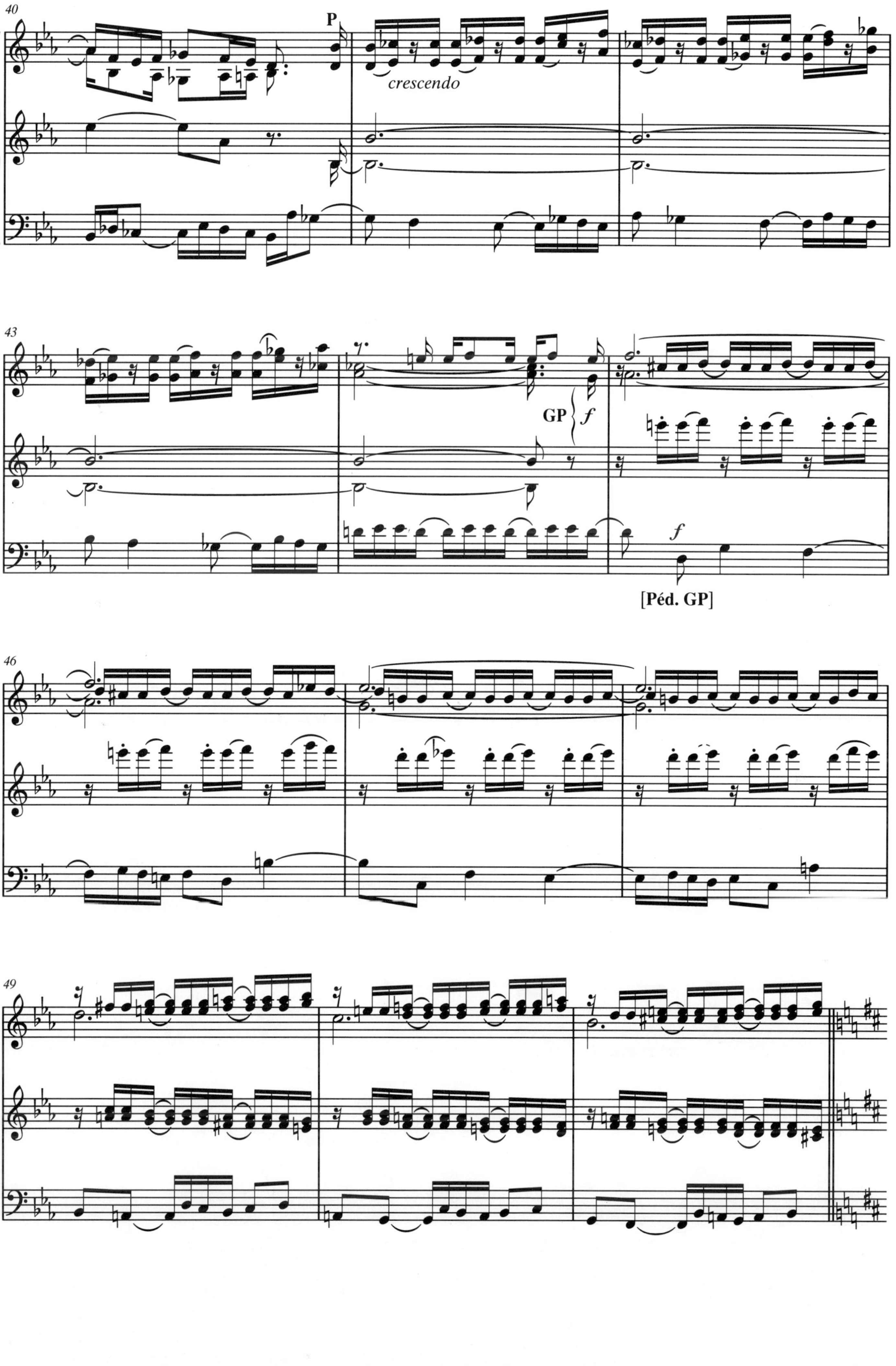
40
P
crescendo
43
GP
f
f
[Péd. GP]
46
49

64

*See Critical Notes, m. 71.

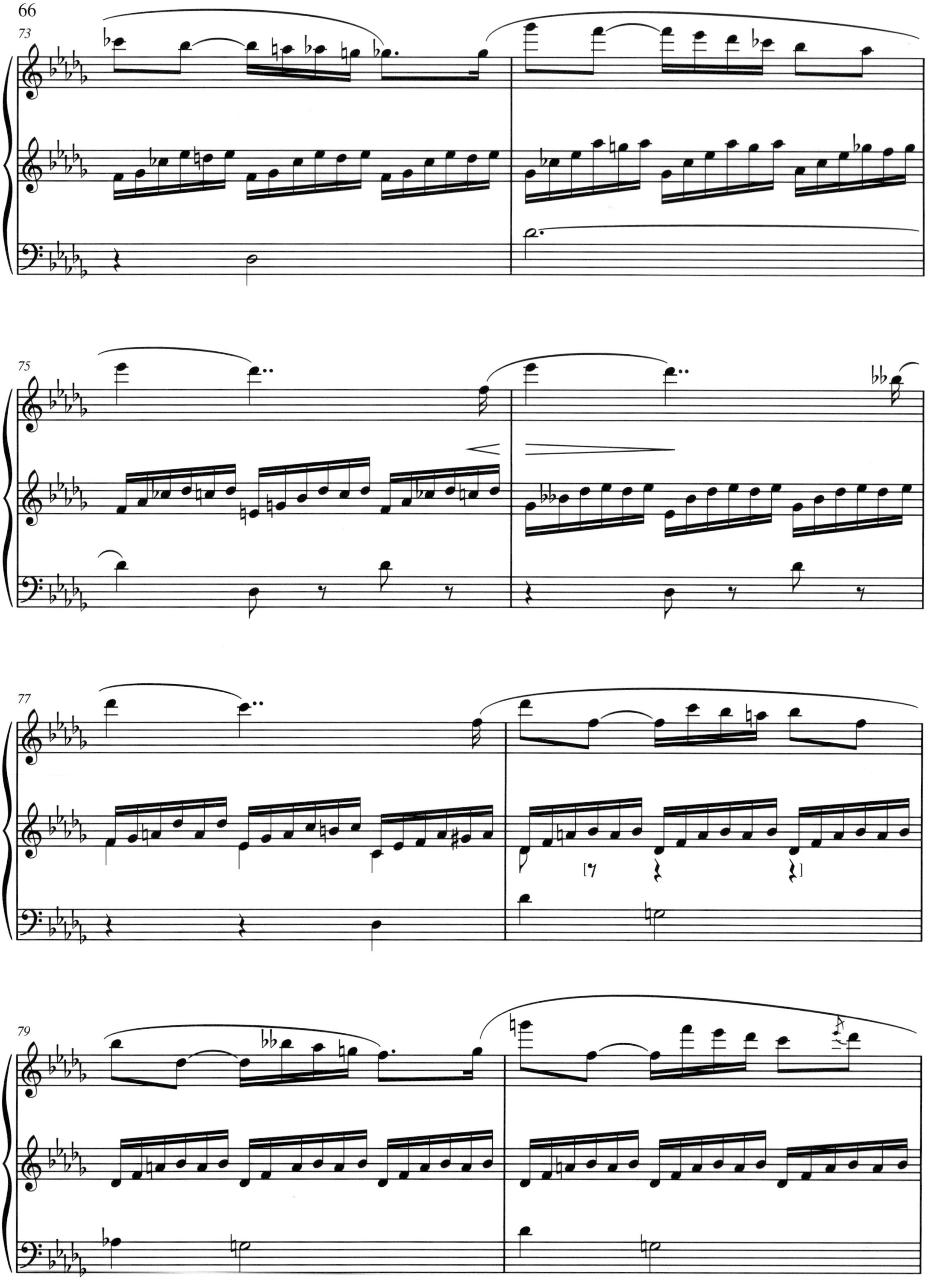
73
75
77
79

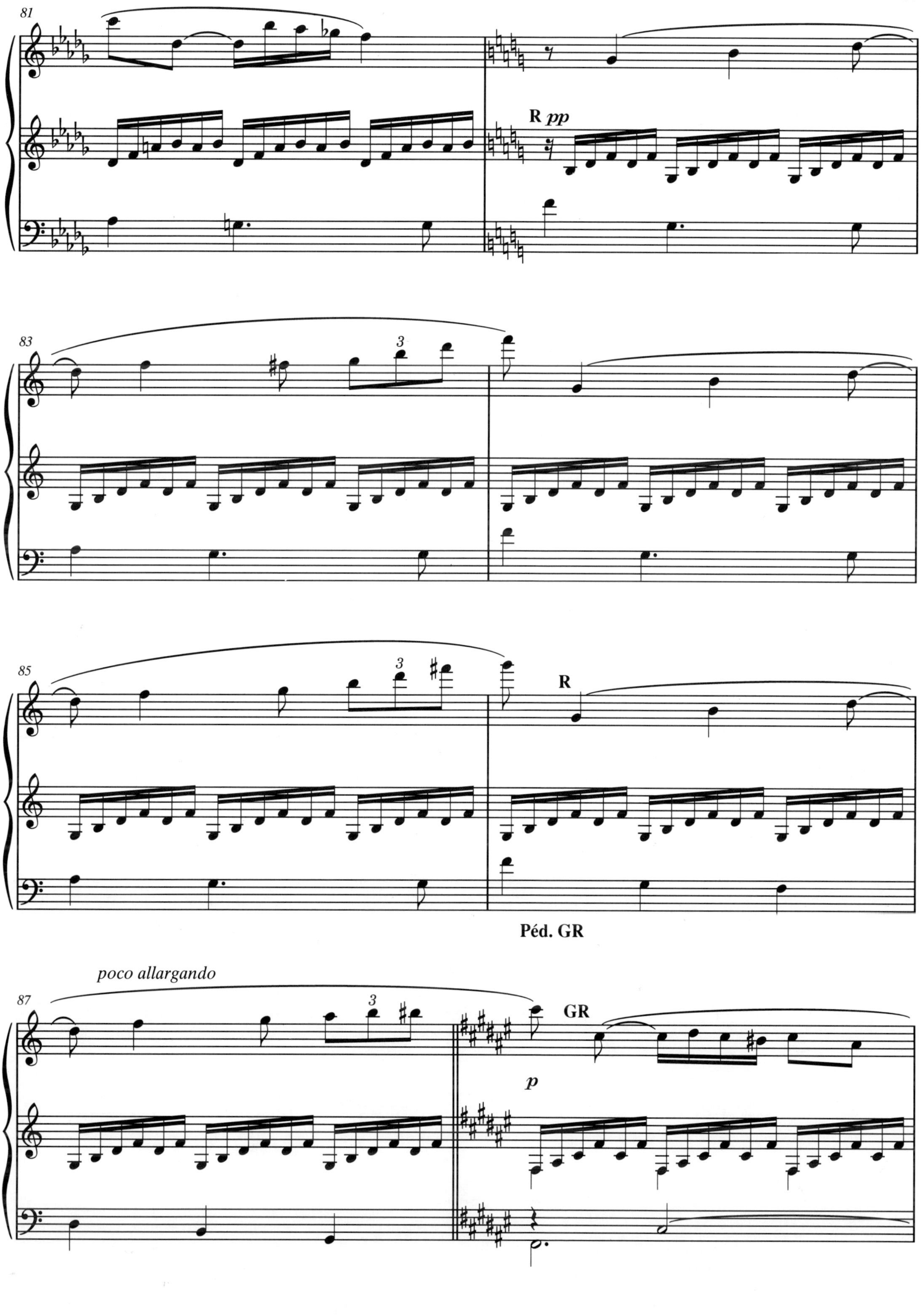
81
R pp
83
85
R
Péd. GR
poco allargando
87
GR
p

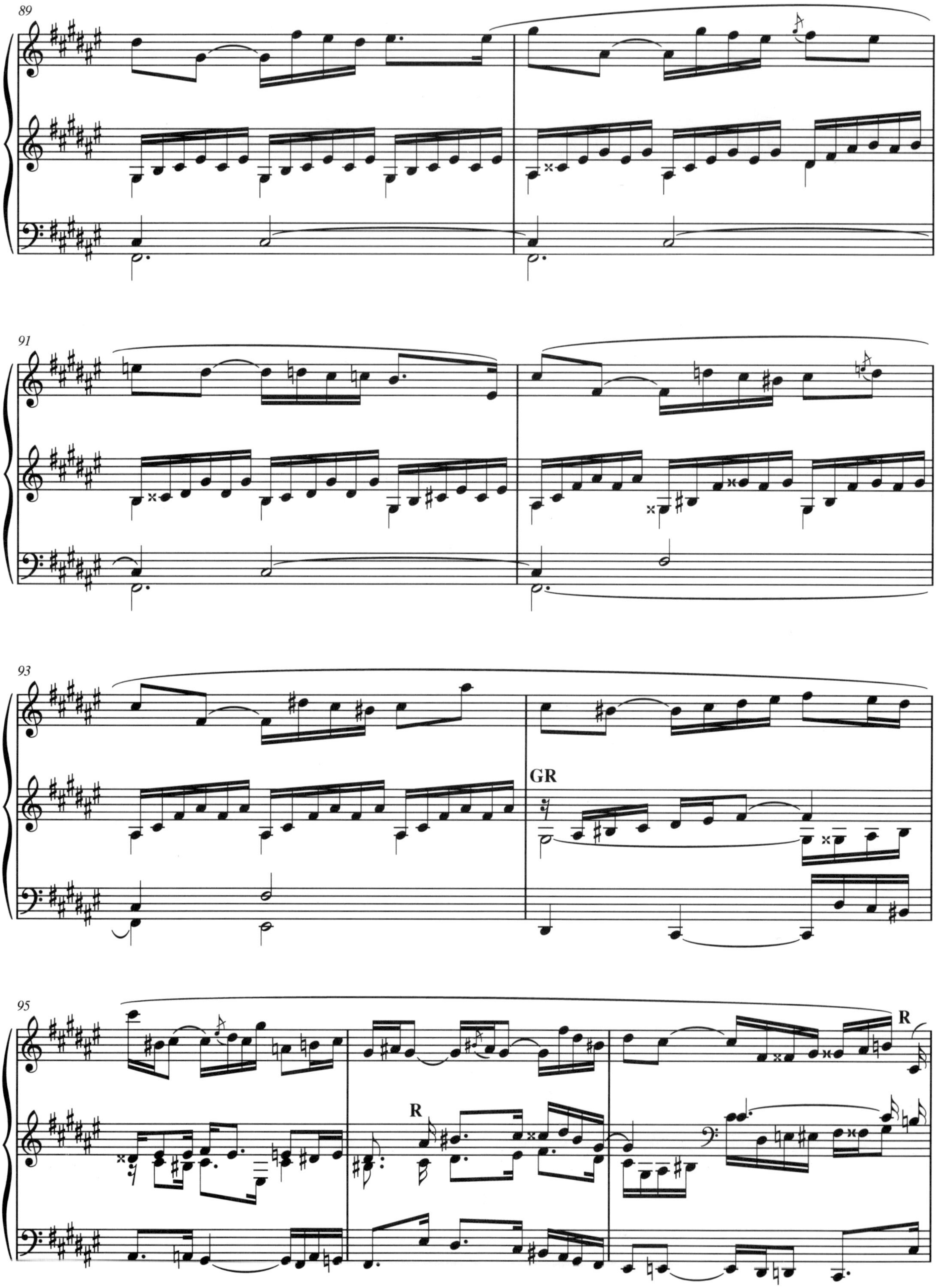
89
91
93
GR
95
R
R

*add

Grand orgue:
Positif:
Recit:
Pédale:

Fonds et Anches 16', 8', 4'

VI. Finale

Tempo giusto ($\quarternote = 96$)

[GPR] fff

[Péd. GPR] fff

71

(Péd. Fonds)

Péd. PR

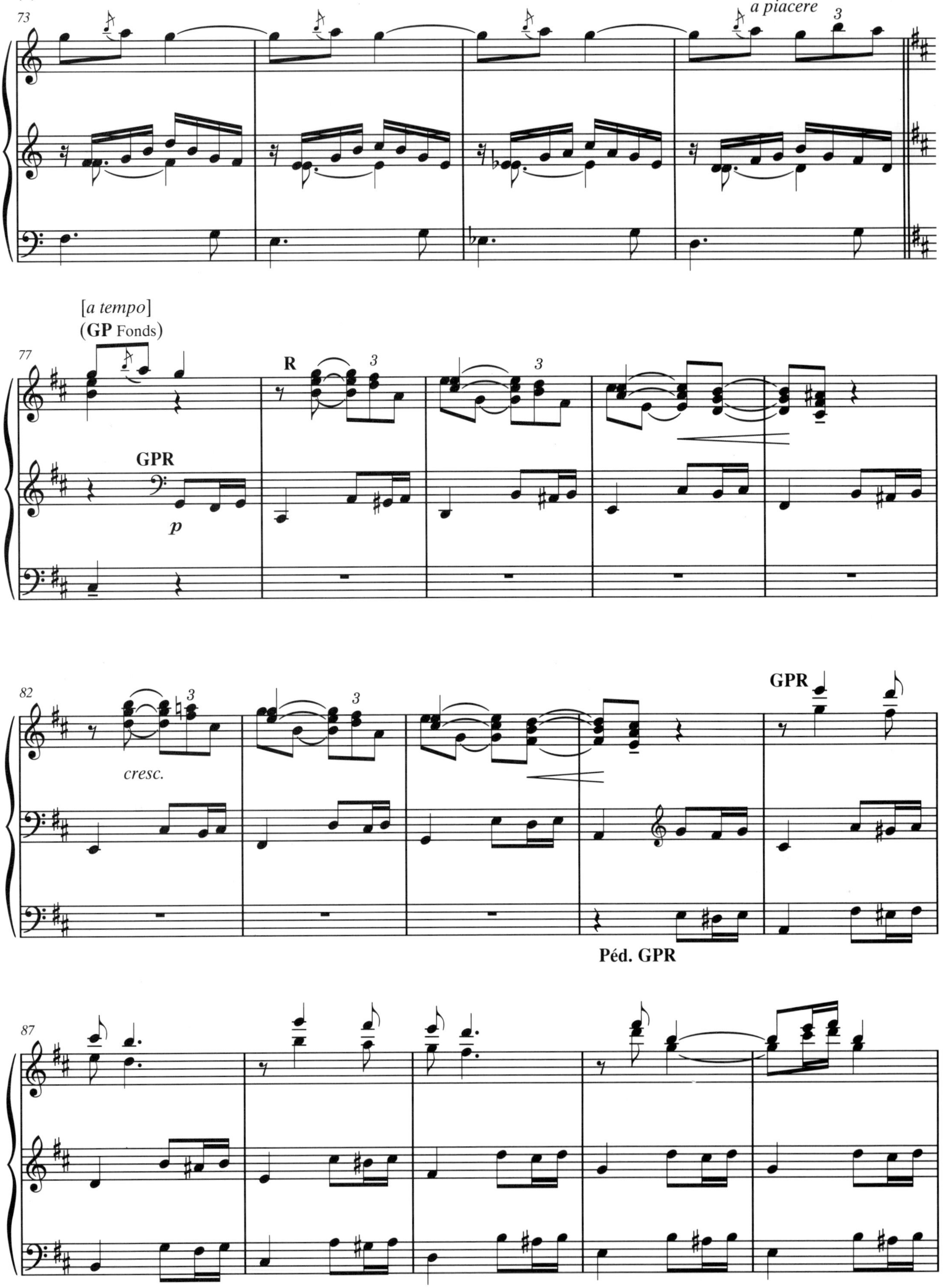
73
a piacere
[a tempo]
(GP Fonds)
77
R
GPR
p
82
cresc.
GPR
Péd. GPR
87

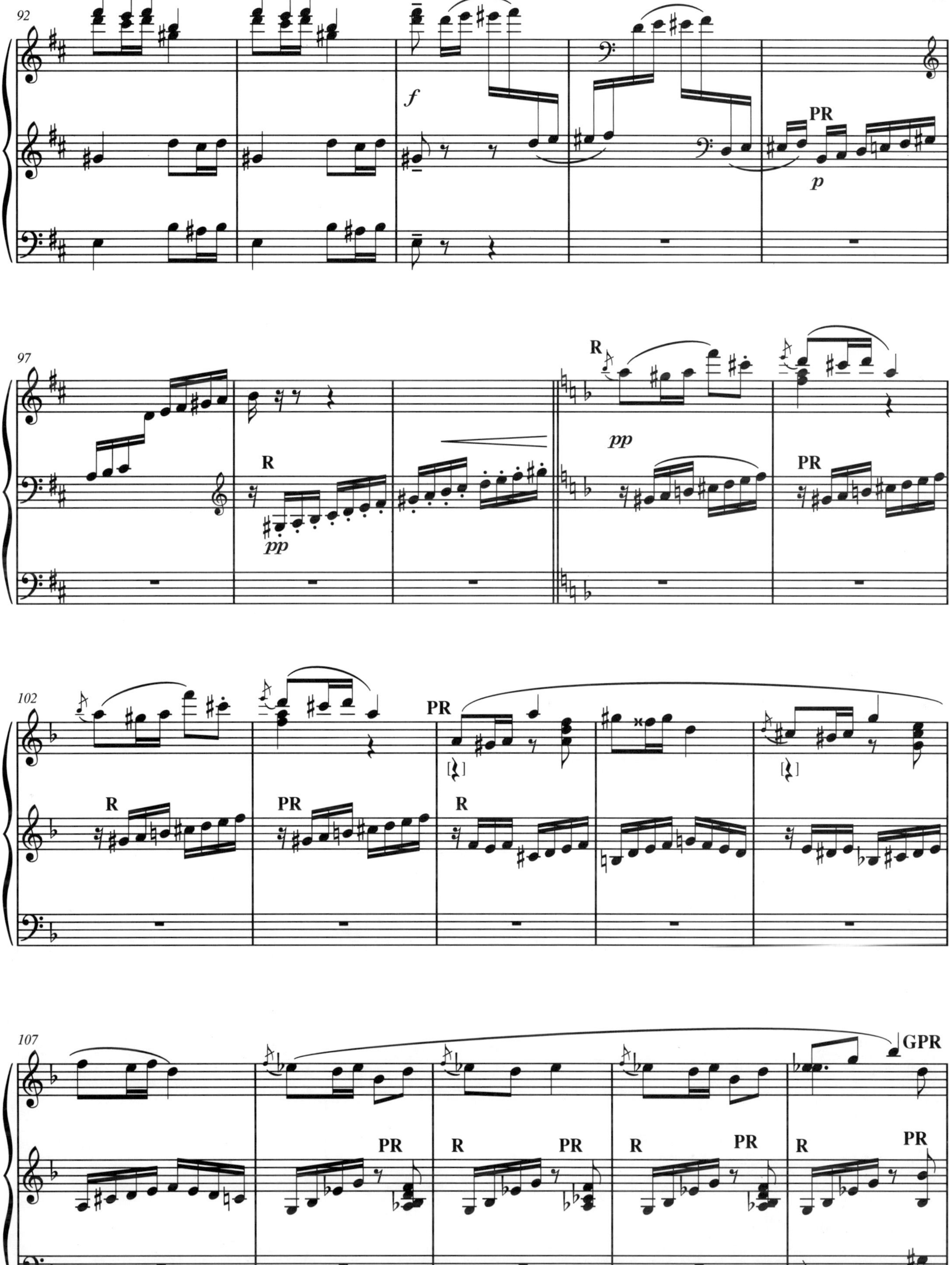
92
f
PR
p
97
R
pp
R
pp
PR
102
R
PR
PR
R
107
PR
R
PR
GPR

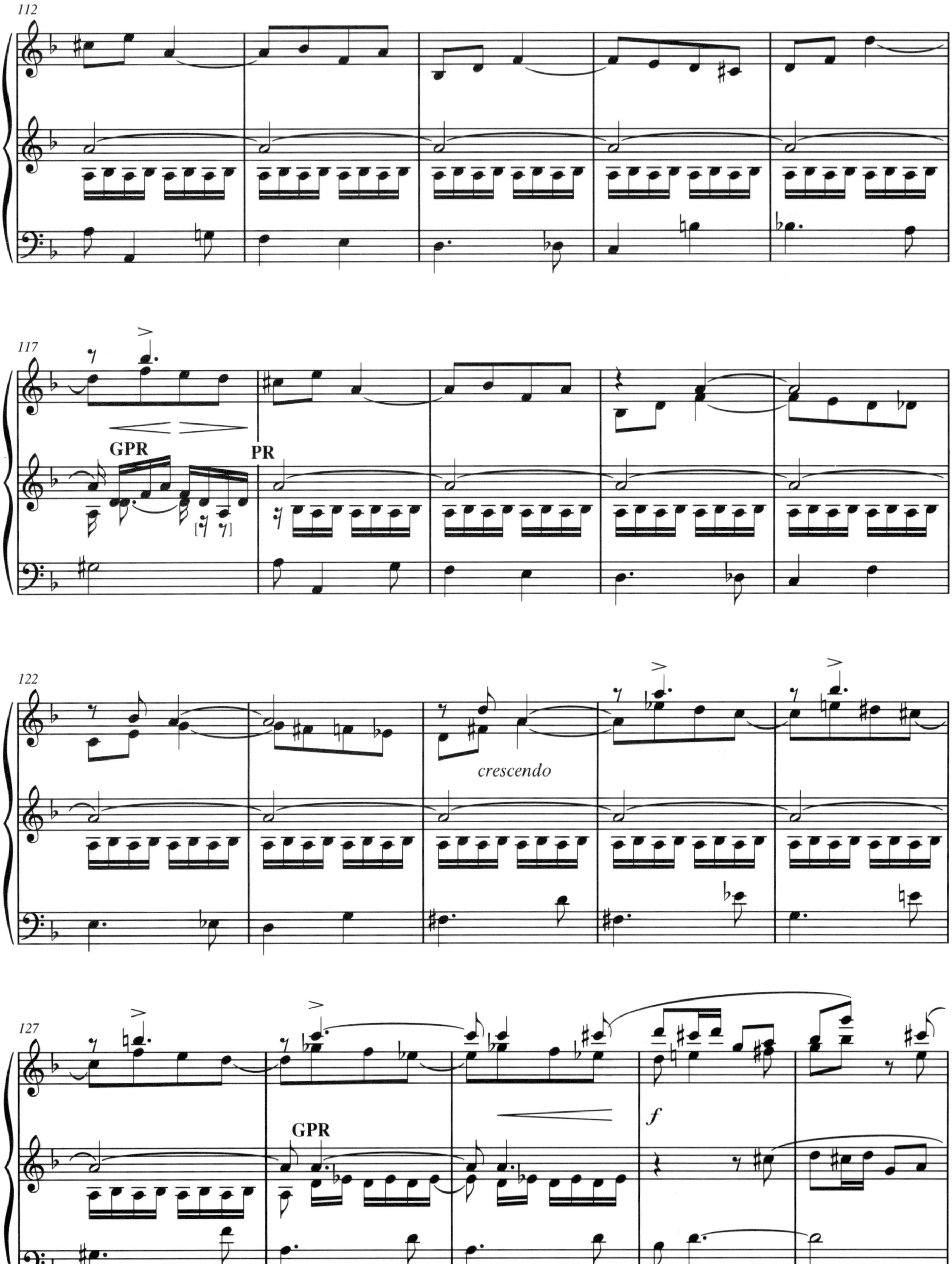
112
117
GPR
PR
122
crescendo
127
GPR
f

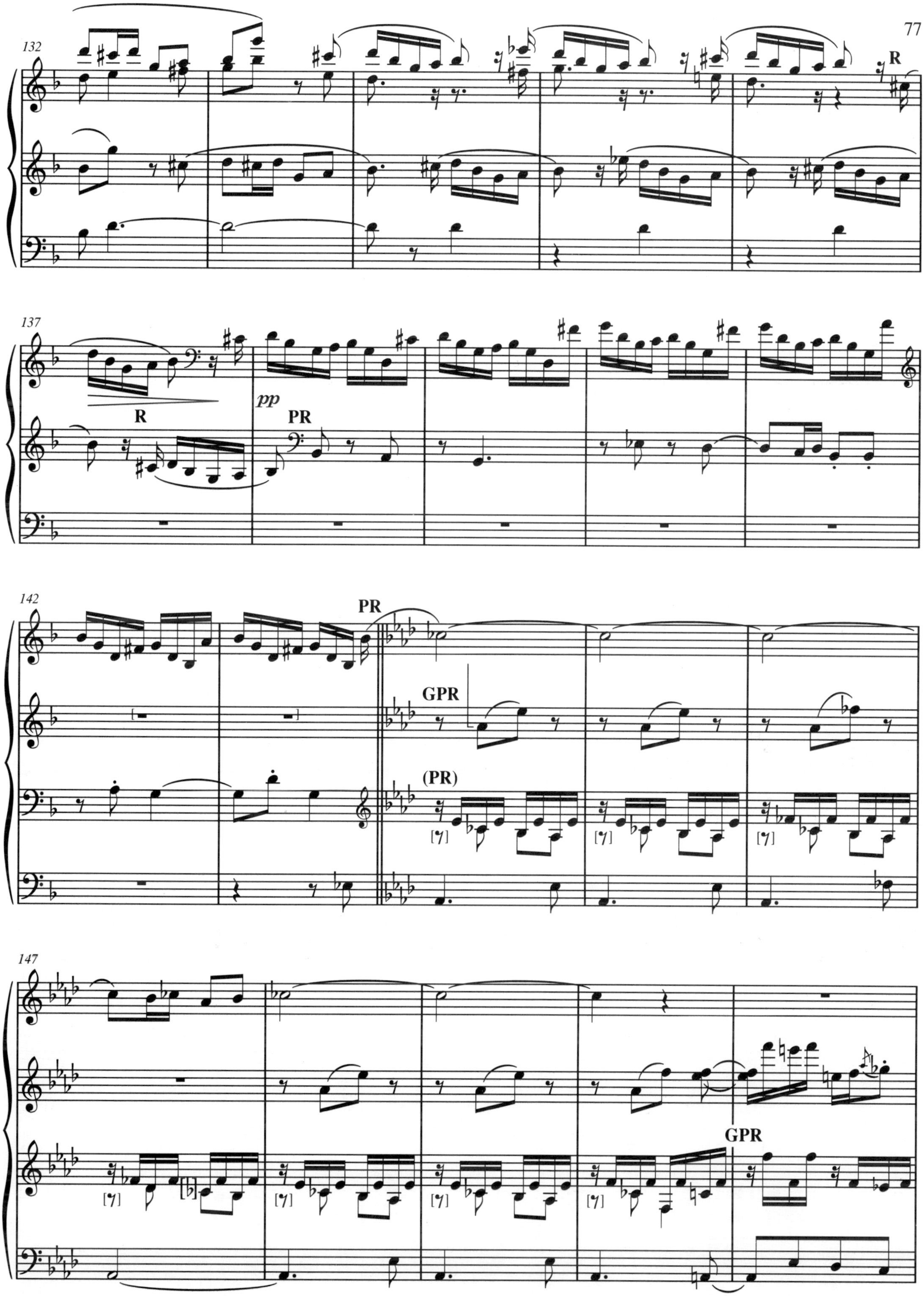
132
R
137
R
pp
PR
142
PR
GPR
(PR)
147
GPR

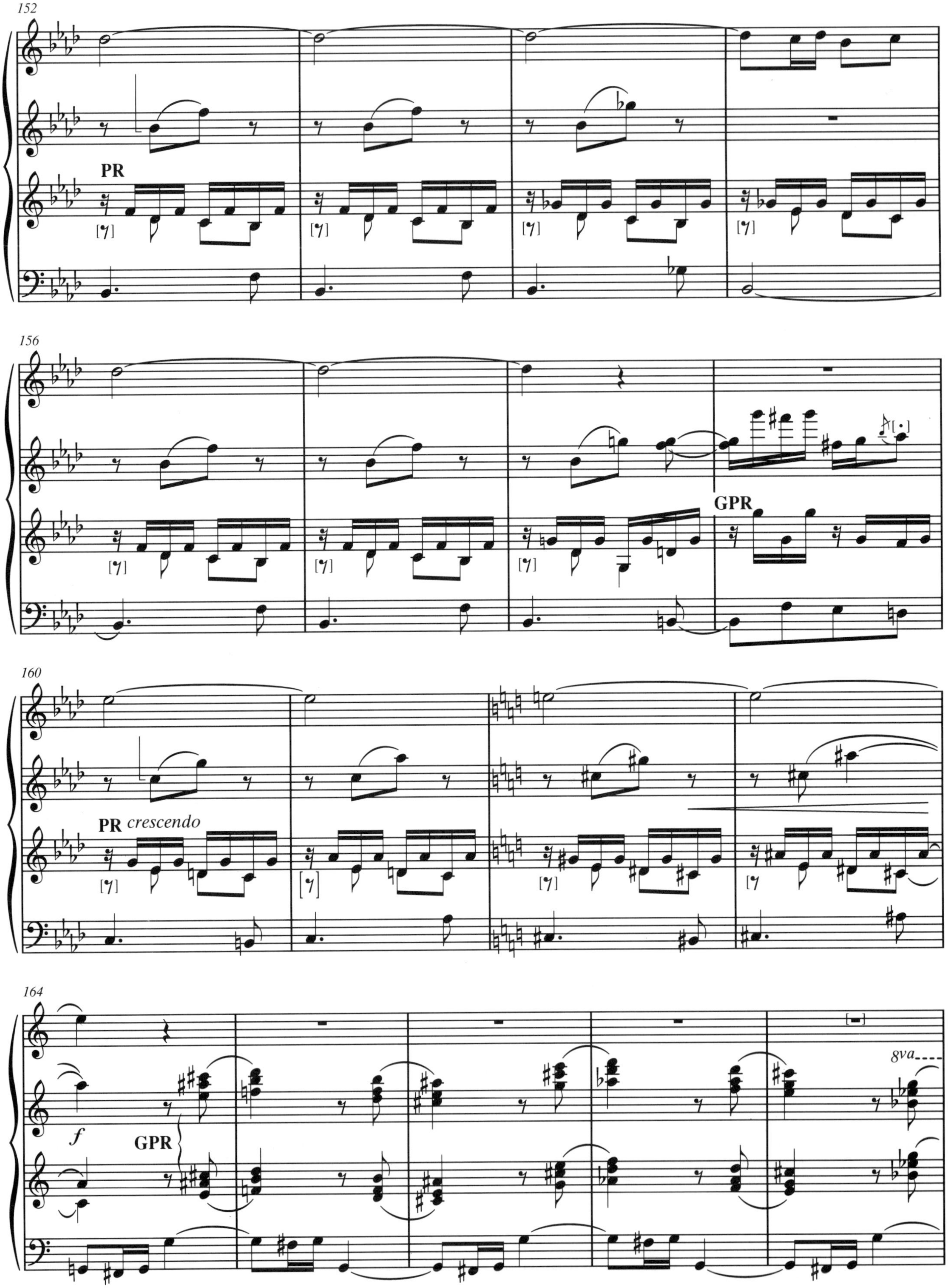
152
PR
156
GPR
160
PR crescendo
164
f
GPR
8va

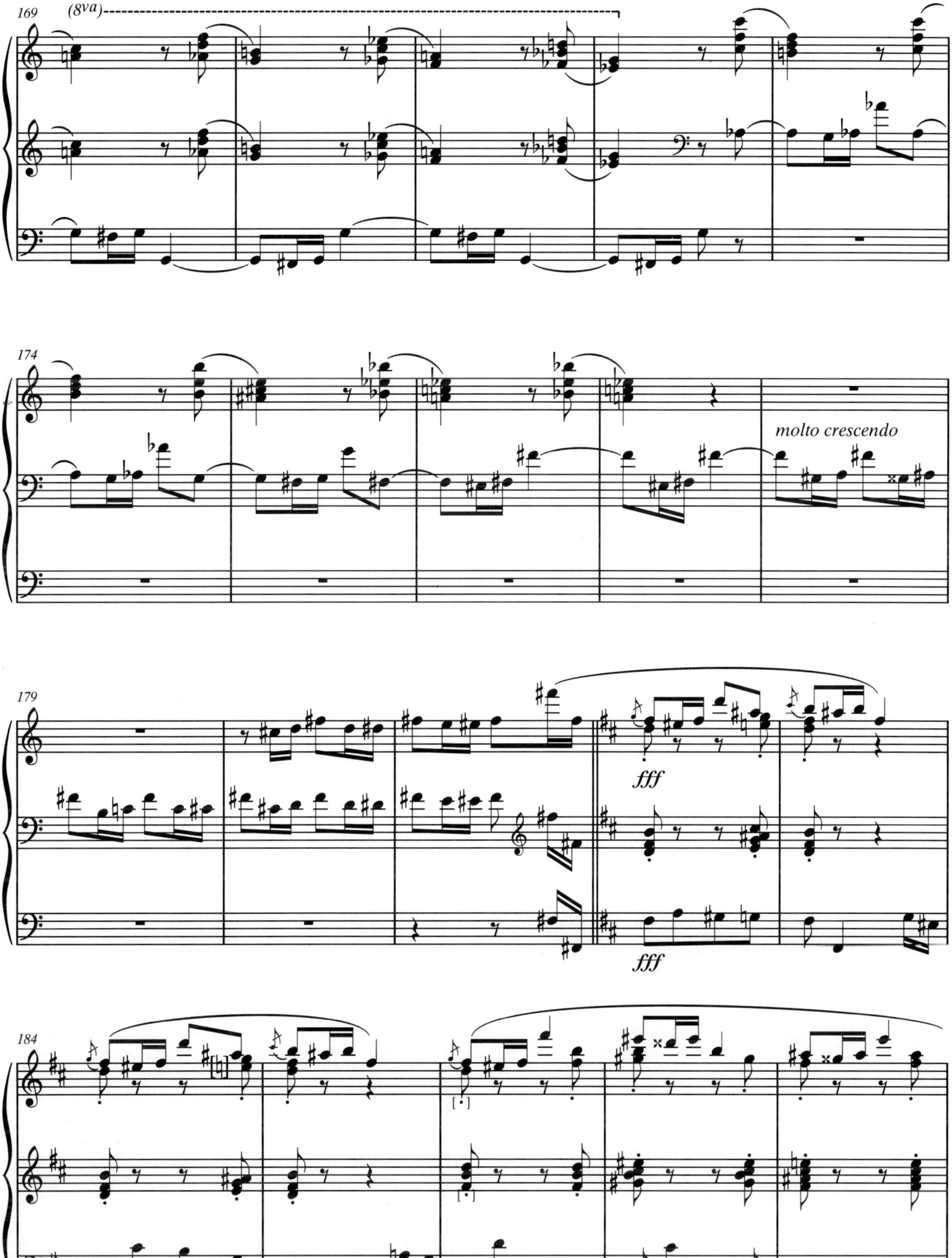
169
(8va)
174
molto crescendo
179
fff
fff
184
[·]
[·]

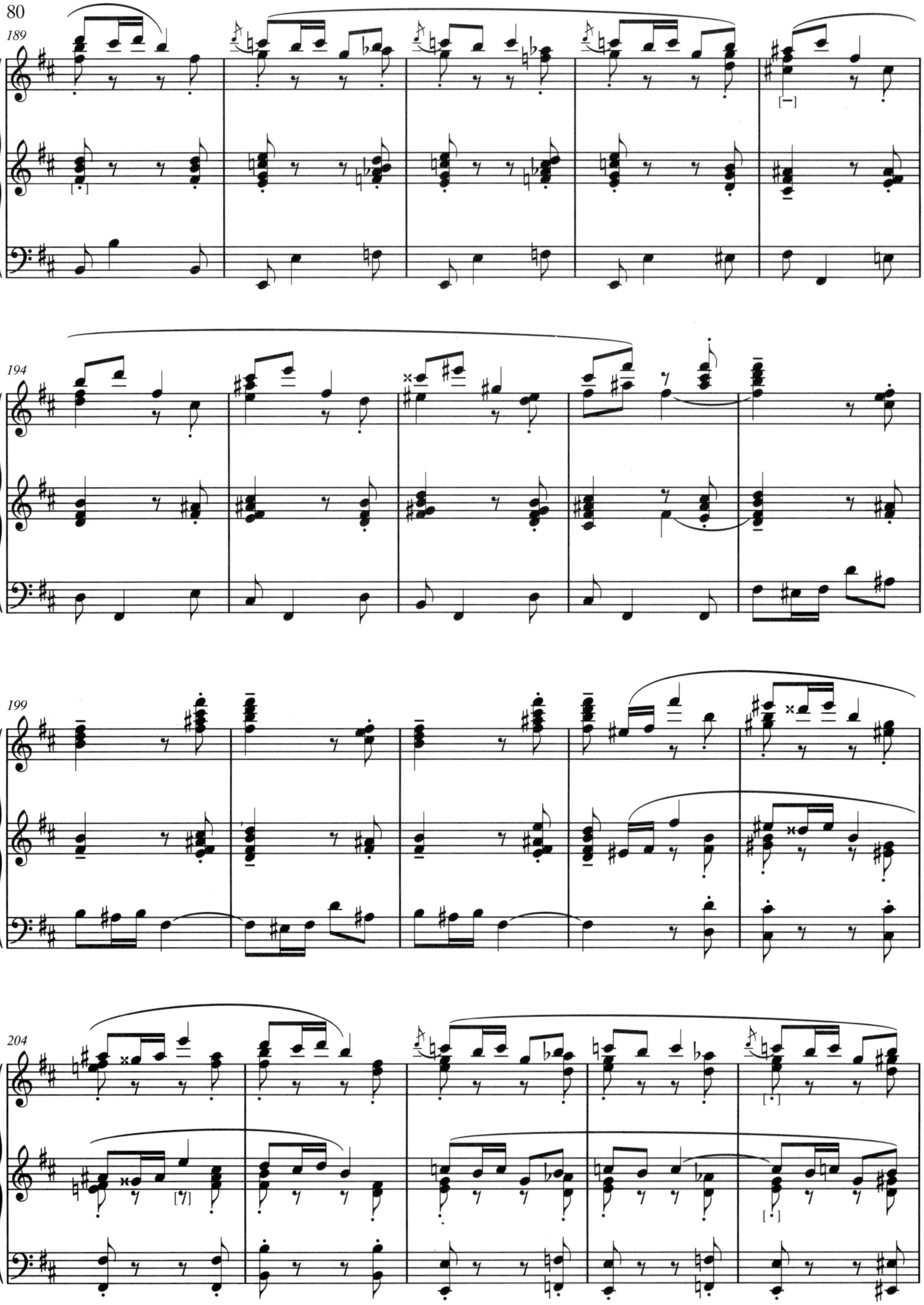
189
194
199
204

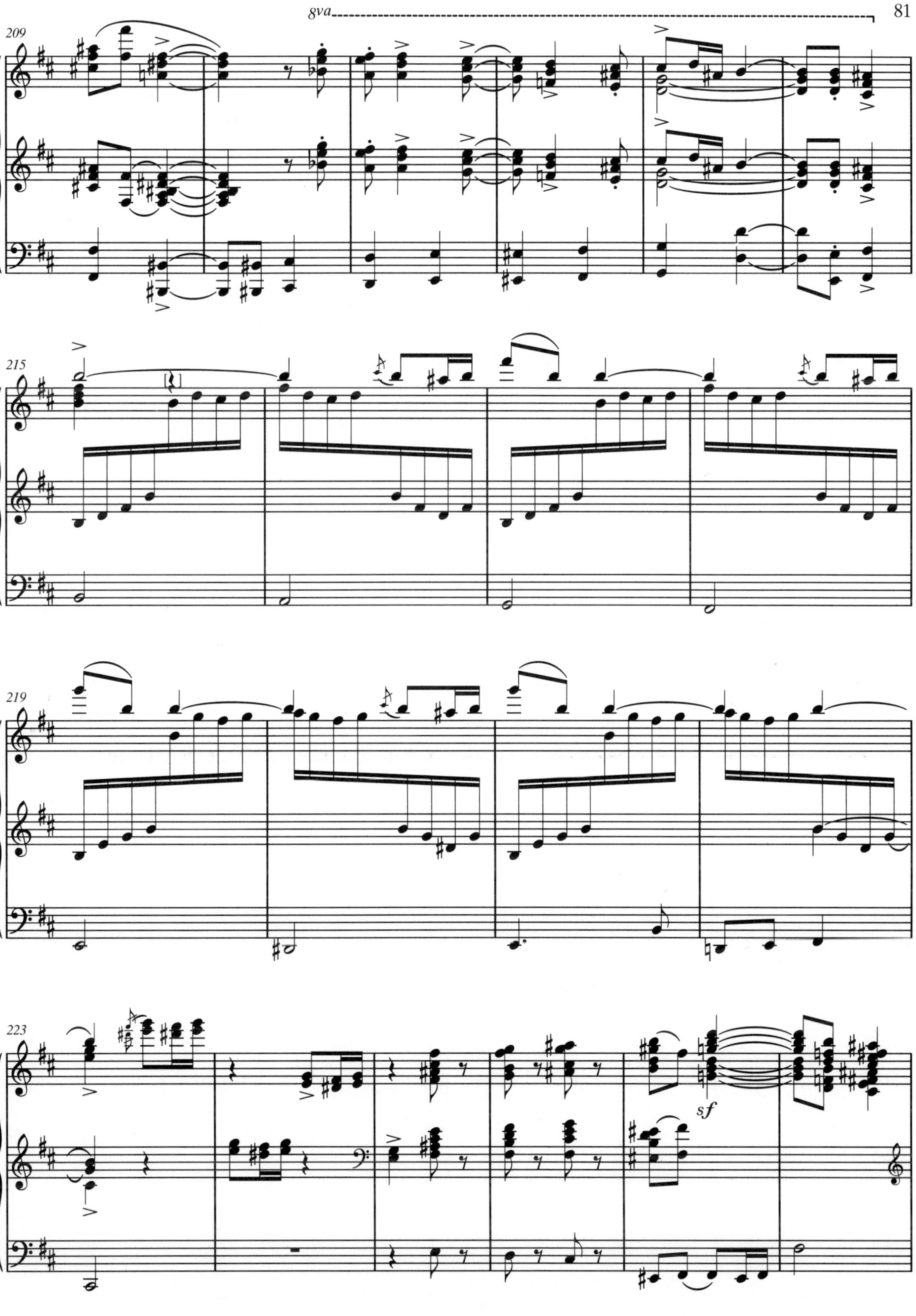
8va
209
215
[ ]
219
223
sf

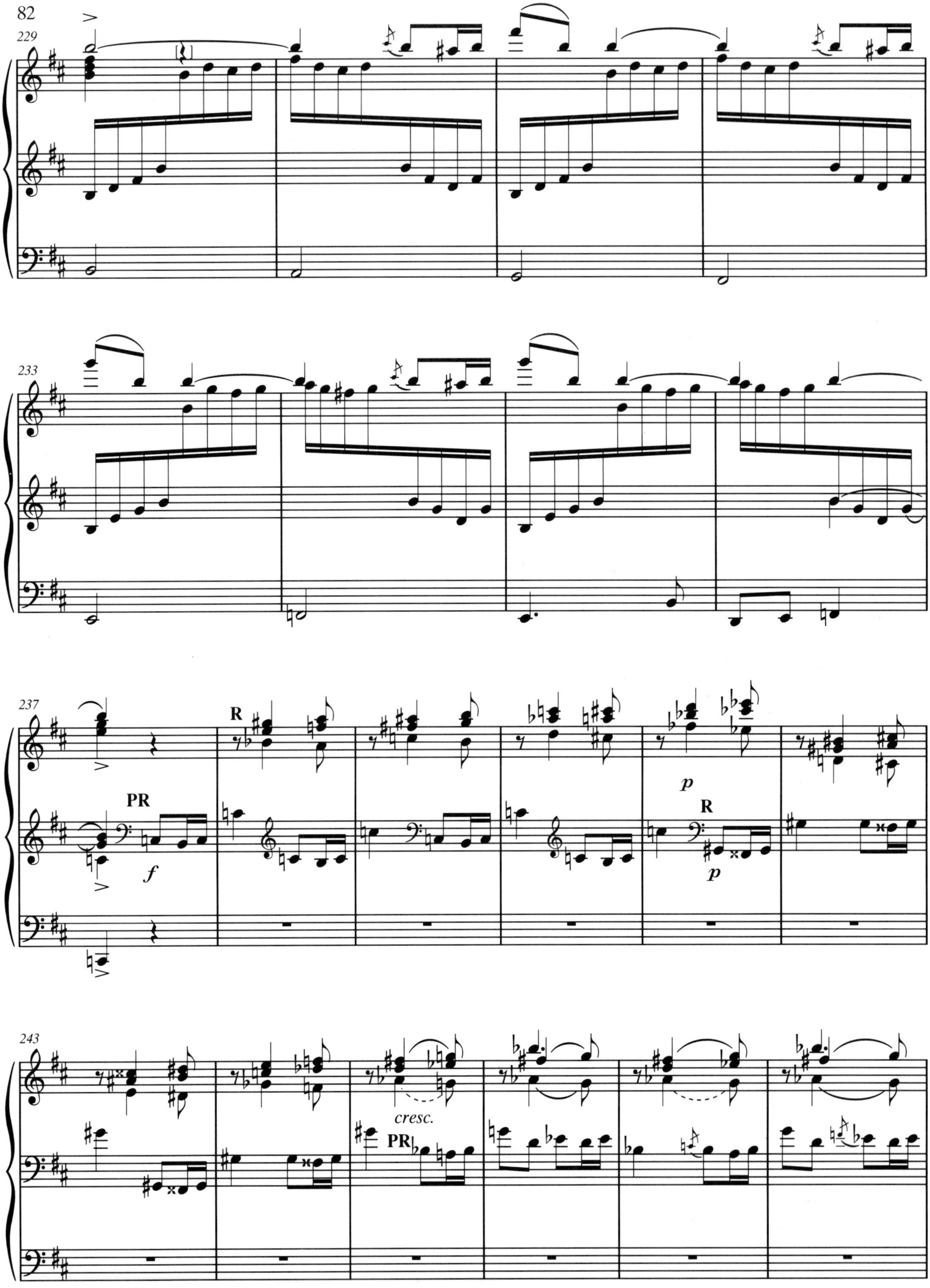
229
233
237
PR
f
R
p
R
p
243
cresc.
PR

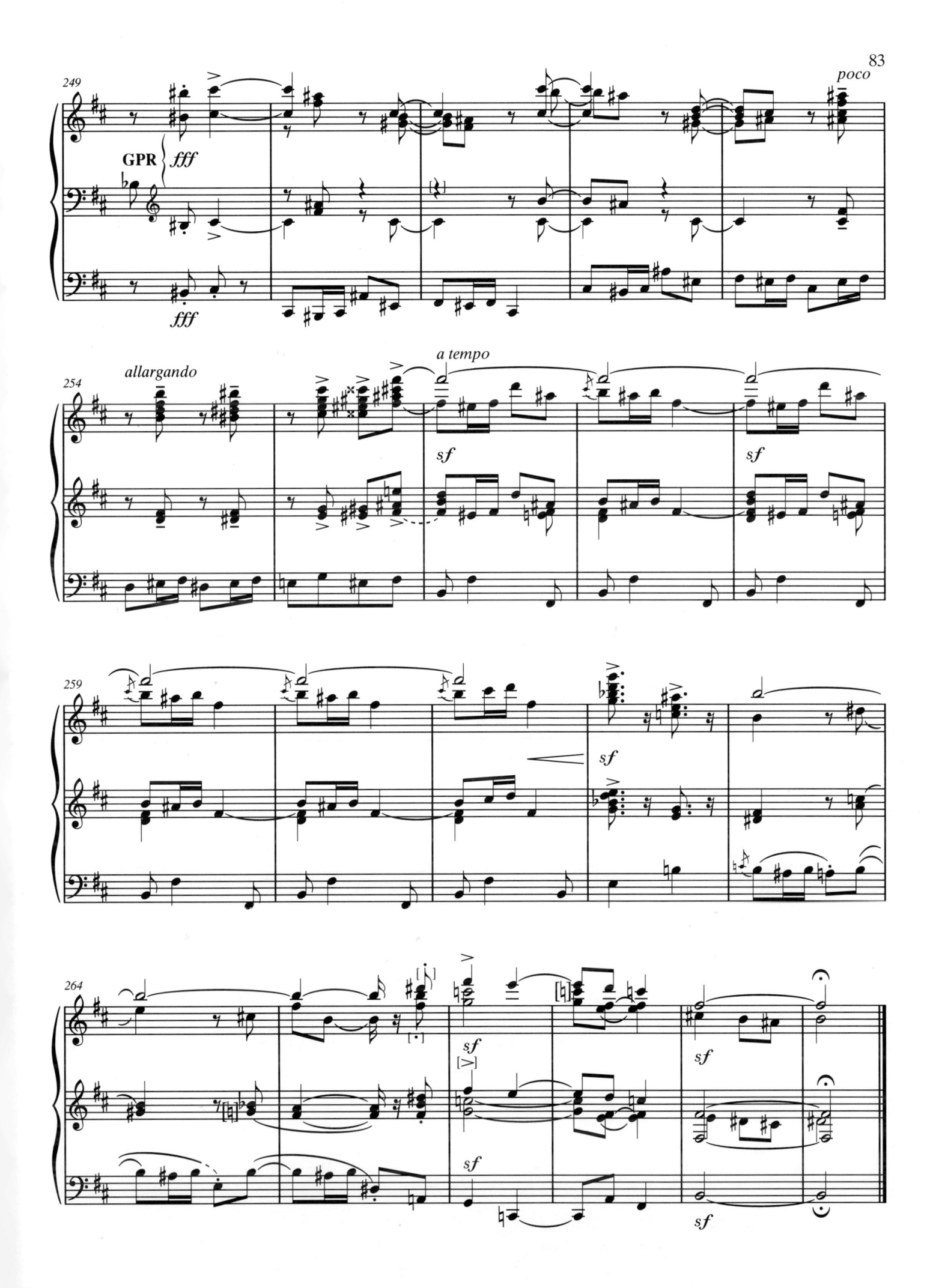
poco
GPR
fff
fff
allargando
a tempo
sf
sf
sf
sf
[>]
sf
sf
sf

Appendix 1

[I]

Editions *B* and *B'*, Mm. 34–40, 52–56, 68–85,
135–38, 146–52, 168–85, 215–20

[Mm. 34–40]*

[Mm. 52–56]†

Edition *B'*:

---

* Editions *B* and *B'*, mm. 34 and 40 = edition *E*, mm. 34 and 39.
† Editions *B* and *B'*, mm. 52 and 56 = edition *E*, mm. 51 and 55.

[Mm. 68–85]*

* Editions *B* and *B'*, mm. 68 and 85 = edition *E*, mm. 67 and 84.

[Mm. 135–38]*

* Editions *B* and *B'*, mm. 135 and 138 = edition *E*, mm. 134 and 137.

[Mm. 146–52]*

[Mm. 168–85]†

* Editions *B* and *B'*, mm. 146 and 152 = edition *E*, mm. 145 and 149.
† Editions *B* and *B'*, mm. 168 and 185 = edition *E*, mm. 165 and 183.

Edition B':

poco ritard.
a tempo

[Mm. 215–20]*

*Editions *B* and *B'*, mm. 215 and 220 = edition *E*, mm. 213 and 218.

Appendix 2

III

Version *B/B′*, Mm. 229–49*

* Version *B/B′*, m. 229 = edition *E*, m. 229.

91

245

Appendix 3
IV. Prélude

Grand orgue: Fonds 16', 8', 4'
Positif: Fonds 16', 8', 4'
Récit: Fonds 16', 8', 4'
Pédale: Fonds 32', 16', 8', 4'

Version *B/B'*

Adagio ($\quarternote = 40$)

poco riten.

GPR f

f

Péd GPR

a tempo

4

R *p*

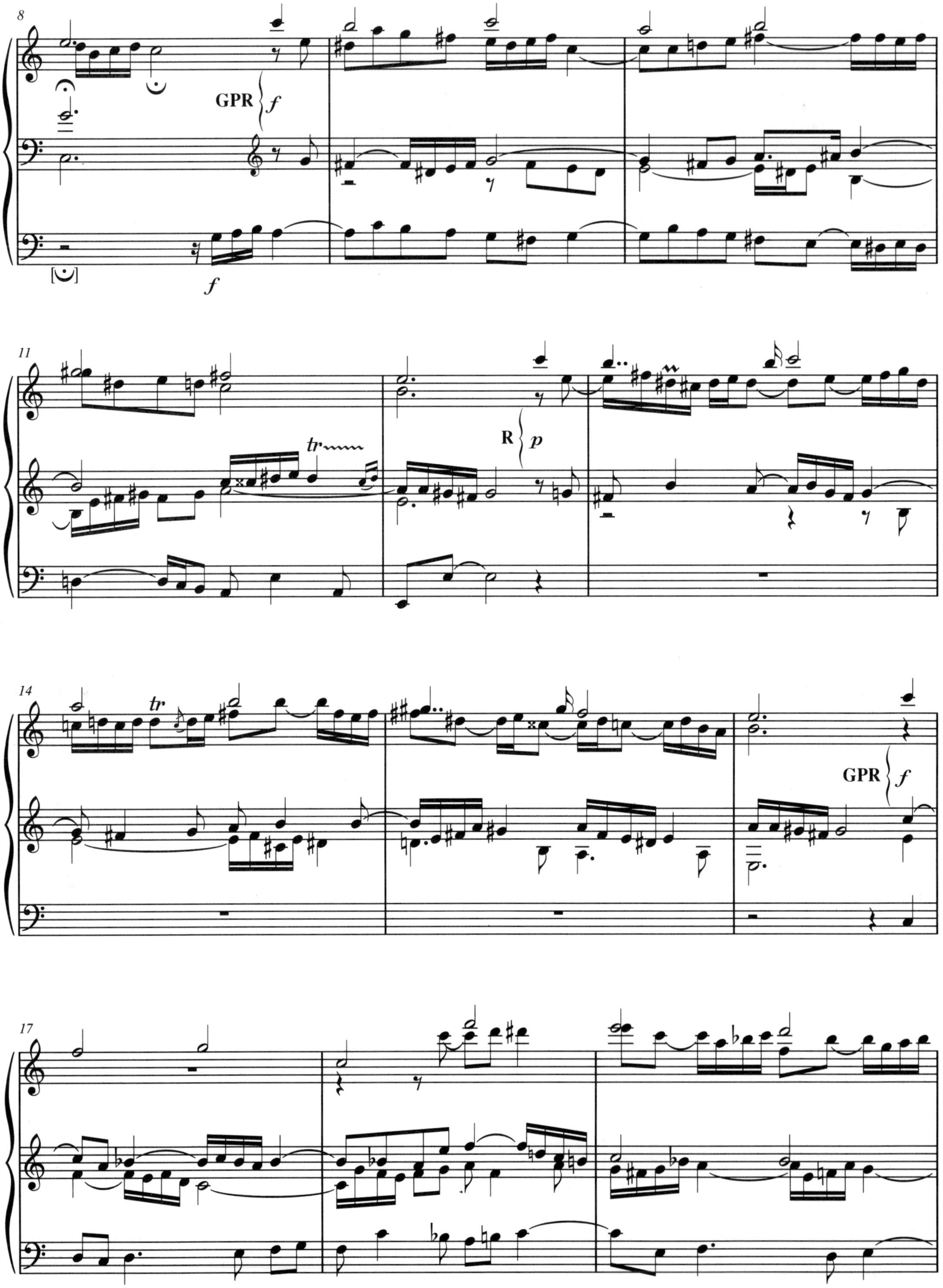
8
GPR
f
f
11
tr
R
p
14
tr
GPR
f
17

20
tr
tr
PR
meno f
23
(R Bourdon 8', Flûte 4')
P
a piacere
meno f
p
(P Flûte 8', Salicional [8'])
27
R
a tempo
p
P
30
rit.

Appendix 4
VII. Finale

Edition *B*, Mm. 261–69*

---

* Edition *B*, m. 261 = version *B'/C/C'/D/E*, m. 261.